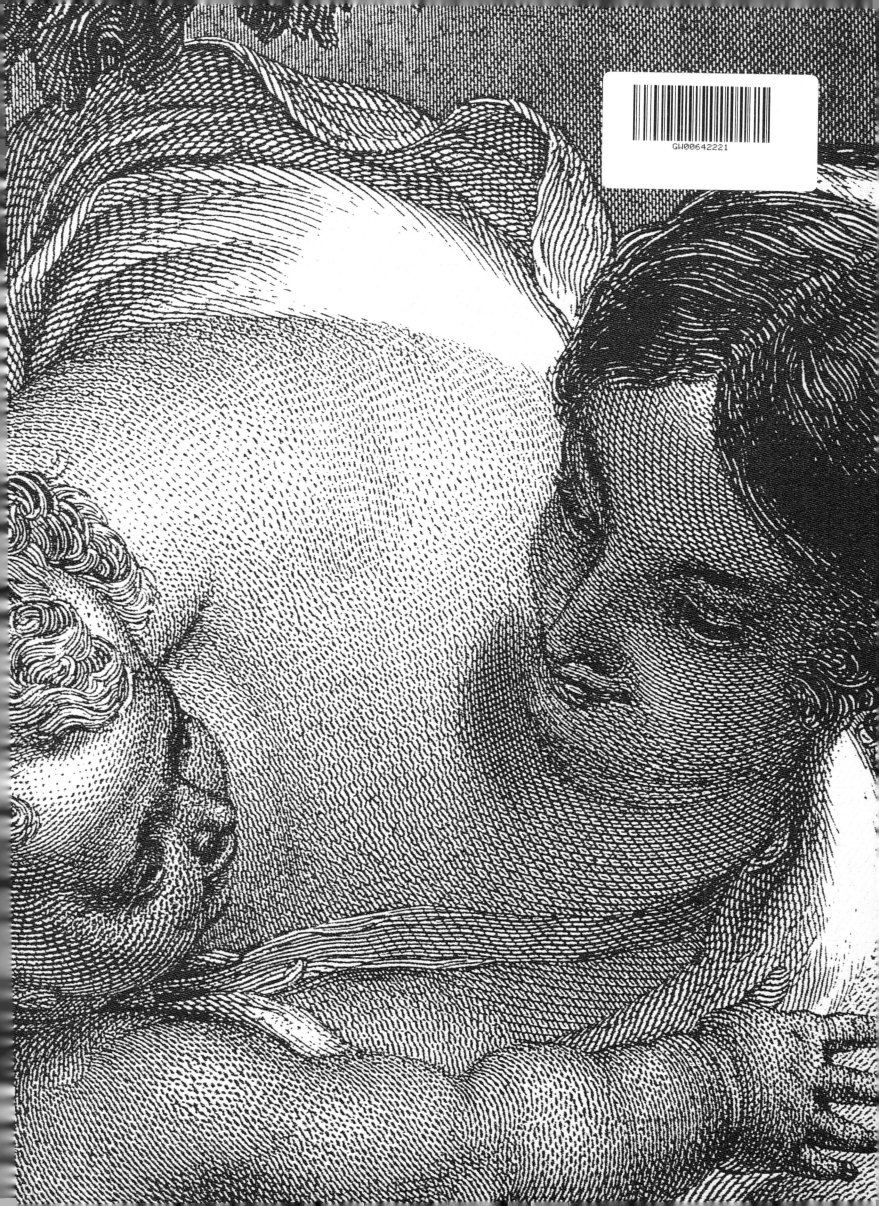

Beautiful embroidery for decoration and display

Kaye Pyke's Sumptuous Settings

Photography by Neil Lorimer

VIKING

To my mother and father,
and to Vannese, for her generosity and style

Viking
Penguin Books Australia Ltd
487 Maroondah Highway, PO Box 257 Ringwood,
Victoria 3134, Australia
Penguin Books Ltd
Harmondsworth, Middlesex, England
Viking Penguin, A Division of Penguin Books USA Inc.
375 Hudson Street, New York, New York 10014, USA
Penguin Books Canada Limited
10 Alcorn Avenue, Toronto, Ontario, Canada M4V 3B2
Penguin Books (N.Z.) Ltd
Cnr Rosedale and Airborne Roads, Albany, Auckland,
New Zealand

First published by Penguin Books Australia Ltd 1997

10 9 8 7 6 5 4 3 2 1

Design by Sandy Cull
Photography by Neil Lorimer
Illustrations by Lisa Moran
Typeset in Belucian by Alena Jencik
Printed and bound by South China Printing Co. Ltd, Hong Kong

National Library of Australia
Cataloguing-in-Publication data

Pyke, Kaye, 1943– .
    Kaye Pyke's sumptuous settings : beautiful embroidery
    for decoration and display.

    Includes index.
    ISBN 0 670 86682 2.

    1. Embroidery – Patterns. 2. Interior decoration.
    I. Title. II. Title: Sumptuous settings.

746.44041

Contents

Introduction

BEAUTIFUL THINGS MATTER TO ME, and sumptuous settings to place them in even more so. My personal space has always been very important, particularly the place that I call home; fashionable clothing comes a poor second to the design and decoration of my living environment. It's important for the interior of my home to look a certain way, and to reflect my style and taste. For example, I love to see exquisite things on show rather than safely hidden away behind cupboard doors. Ideally, they would be useful everyday things as well: a cup and saucer for that first coffee every morning, a vase for flowers from my garden,

I would drift through galleries looking at paintings, lingering over the background and setting details. When I went to the movies, again I paid more attention to the settings than to the storyline!

a bowl for fruit on the kitchen bench. I always choose items for my home that are a delight to look at, and that give me pleasure.

I am especially passionate about eighteenth-century European interiors. I suspect this came from a childhood girlfriend's mother who made a great impression on me with her wonderful *savoir faire*. I used to love staying at their home on weekends, wandering through the rooms filled with antiques, china, beautiful fabrics and, always, bowls of vibrant flowers. I would also drift through galleries looking at paintings, lingering over the background and setting details. When I went to the movies, again I think I paid more attention to the settings than to the storyline!

At home, where I shared a bedroom with my sister, my side of the room was always crowded with the things I had collected. I remember taking wooden fruit boxes and stacking them, one on top of the other, to make shelves. 'Curtains' hung from either side, and I was constantly arranging and rearranging my little ceramic and plaster of Paris bits and pieces.

After I got married and had my first baby, I took up sewing tapestries, but I soon tired of following someone else's designs and using the same stitch over and over. I began designing my own embroideries and making cushions. Friends admired them and wanted to learn how to make them, and so my embroidery classes began, at first in my sitting room at home, then later in my decorating and embroidery boutique in Bay Street, Port Melbourne.

Today, I no longer sell decorating and gift items, and my shop is purely an embroidery boutique where I specialise in fabrics, yarns, threads, braids and ribbons – everything you could possibly need for a project. The shop has been redecorated, and now has pale French grey walls with gold cornices. They make an elegant match for the mirror frames that hang at either end of the room. Antique French armoires and cabinets hold the fabrics, ribbons and braids, just as in the old passementerie boutiques in the back streets of Paris.

I love to see exquisite things on show rather than safely hidden away.

Kaye Pyke's Sumptuous Settings covers many aspects of decoration and display and features fine objects that I love, including cushions, pictures and trimmings. Embroidered and matching decorator cushions are such an easy way of adding vivacity to an existing colour scheme. I have included detailed instructions for 29 cushions and pictures, and some, such as Julia's Rose Cushion (pages 86–89) and Cream Carnation Posy Cushion (pages 99–101), reveal new flowers.

I have divided the book into four thematic chapters. Chapter one, 'All That Glitters', deals with my love of all things in gold and gilt, and features embroidery that takes its inspiration from the Baroque. Chapter two, 'A Unique Harmony', explores ways of mixing and matching various forms, shapes, patterns and motifs, and looks at how the seemingly impossible – for example, a piece of petit point paired with ocelot linen – can *I urge the use of weird and wonderful combinations of colours and fabrics.* produce stunning results. Chapter three, 'For the Love of Flowers', is an ode to the gorgeousness of flowers, which I think needs little introduction! And in chapter four, 'Rustlings of Romance', you'll get a glimpse of my bedroom, and of other romance-inspired projects and settings.

I urge the use of weird and wonderful combinations of colours and fabrics. Keep experimenting with new and different blends of fabrics – they often produce interesting results that at first glance might seem to clash. As you will see in chapter two, differences in texture, weight, colour, print, and even the watermark on moiré fabric will produce stunning effects. I often use different dye lots when making up cushions, so that the frills and background fabric don't quite match.

ABOVE TOP: *Of all my mirrors, this is my favourite. It comes from Paris and would once have been placed on the stairway landing so that householders could check their appearance before greeting their guests. The woman in the portrait reminds me so much of my mother.* ABOVE: *This sofa in my sitting room is covered in ocelot print linen. I had several cushions of different shapes made up with the left-over fabric, including the edging on the faux wolf throw rug.*

And while most people prefer pastel colours, I love bright and vibrant tones. I am always encouraging my students to be more daring in their choice of colour. I hope the colours of the Fuchsia Velvet Rose (pages 49–51), Polka Dot Posy (pages 56–59) and French Blue cushions (pages 80–85) will inspire even the most reserved of embroiderers to lash out and try something a little more daring!

I invariably choose upholstery-weight fabrics for their hard-wearing capacity, as well as for their stability. They are strong enough to resist stretching out of shape as you embroider. I also like to work with silks and pleated silks, brocades, damasks, moiré fabrics, taffetas, tapestries, and organzas. I still use calico, which was the fabric I first started embroidering with, and I often use gingham for a more casual, country feel.

Don't throw out old fabrics – they are ideal to have on hand to use and re-use. To me, the more worn and faded a fabric becomes, the more interesting it is. Signs of age give a fabric history and a sense of a previous life that appeal to me. The Ivana Trump Cushion (pages 95–97), for example, is made from a grey-blue

Transforming your home need not be an expensive exercise – all it takes is enthusiasm, a clear idea of the look you're after, and some lateral thinking. The cheapest unbleached calico can be made into eye-catching Austrian blinds. Scour auction rooms for items no-one else seems interested in; some creative application will usually breathe new life into an existing piece of furniture. Save up scraps and remnants of fabrics to put together cushions. If you buy the things you love, you'll be able to build up collections with ease, and you'll find that each piece will more or less work with everything else.

ABOVE: *I adore this old Louis XVI-style chair with its tattered underbelly. Beside it is a Florentine cabinet set with a range of collectables, including a candlestick that holds a dried rosebud shade made by Chyka Keebaugh, whose work and ideas I greatly admire.* BELOW: *The pale pink, full-blown roses on this side table were hand-painted by an artist friend, Jane Devine. Everything on top of it complements their graceful splendour, from the delicate creamy roses – freshly gathered from my own tiny garden – to the miniature portrait of a woman attached to the top of the ornate mirror.*

silk that was once a set of bathroom curtains. When I took them apart, I found that some of the fabric had faded to a pale green. I used these for the frill. It's a shame to discard such lovely fabric; the marks and fading make it more interesting than when pristine and new. Sometimes, using a fabric inside out will also give an aged, unusual look. This is particularly true of damasks.

Before you start any project, remember that the right materials are needed to achieve the desired effect. For example, ribbon roses can't be made with just any old ribbon: they need to be soft and supple with a glow of colour about them. New ribbons are often made from polyester, which is too stiff and shiny to be worked into embroidered flowers. Ribbons for making roses also need to be double-sided so that they can be twisted and turned into the required shapes. I find older and antique ribbons produce more satisfactory results. You really can't afford to be thrifty when it comes to fine embroidery – it takes hours of stitching to produce each piece, and the time is wasted if you've used second-grade materials. For this

I have tried to capture some of the exquisite femininity, and the charm, glamour and exoticism of the Baroque.

timber, and indulgently finished with voluptuous curves. There is a smattering of splendid gilded furnishings, and beautifully carved and ornate mirror and picture frames that provide graceful touches.

These touches also come from the lighting, which so generously affords its own natural gilt. I dislike overhead lighting, preferring table lamps and side lamps for effect. Candles and candlesticks also work very well, producing a soft, diffused glow. Mirrors placed at strategic points will capture the light of candles and lamps, or reflections of pictures and paintings. They also make a room appear much lighter and larger than it actually is. The frames of my mirrors and pictures are usually heavy and quite ornate, in keeping with my fondness for eighteenth-century *objets d'art*.

All the gilt and glitter in the world are useless if they do not reveal some of the character, personality and dreams of the person who lives there.

Auction rooms and second-hand shops are great places at which to pick up ornamental pieces that might otherwise be unaffordable. Don't worry too much if it's not the real thing; a well-presented reproduction piece can look just as good. I've found some wonderful mirror and picture frames at trash 'n' treasure markets that with a touch of gilding have ended up looking fabulous.

All the gilt and glitter in the world are useless if they do not reveal some of the character, personality and dreams of the person who lives there; however, there is a fine line between having some gilt and glitter in a room and having too much. Some gilded picture frames, a little brass edging on furniture, or perhaps even an antique gilt candelabra are enough. Establish your own balance.

Girl with Cavalier Damask Cushion

The centrepiece of this cushion is an Italian silk portrait of a young lady. It's edged with fine gold braid and stands on a gold bullion cut-out as though it were a picture in a frame. Silk ribbon roses in shades of pink set off the picture at the bottom and at the top. The gold ribbons and braids are from Bell'Occhio, a shop in San Francisco that specialises in antique trims.

EMBROIDERY MATERIALS

50 cm (20 in) square beige damask

1 large silk picture

1 reel gold thread

small piece of antique gold mesh fabric or tulle

2 m (2.2 yd) antique gold cord

3 m (3.3 yd) silk ribbon no. 65 (dusty pink),
    7 mm (⅓ in) wide

2 m (2.2 yd) silk ribbon no. 34 (beige), 7 mm
    (⅓ in) wide

25 cm (10 in) silk ribbon no. 5 (pale pink),
    7 mm (⅓ in) wide

4 m (4.4 yd) silk ribbon no. 143 (bronze green),
    4 mm (³⁄₁₆ in) wide

1 skein DMC stranded cotton no. 830
    (bronze green)

ASSEMBLY MATERIALS

1.5 m (1.6 yd) gold ribbon, 40 mm (1½ in) wide

1.5 m (1.6 yd) antique gold fringing

3 m (3.3 yd) gold braid

1   Cut out a piece of damask measuring 47 × 40 cm (18½ × 16 in). Trace the design onto the centre of the fabric in pencil.

2   Trim the silk picture into an oval shape and tack onto the fabric with gold thread.

3   Cut out the gold mesh fabric into the shape of the crest below the silk picture. Tack down with gold thread.

4   Take a 75 cm (29½ in) piece of antique gold cord and tie a bow in the centre. Stitch into place at the top of the cameo and tack down the tails of the bow around the edge of the silk print using gold thread. Stitch down the gold cord around the shape of the crest using a tacking stitch in gold thread.

5   Make 10 ribbon roses using the dusty pink silk ribbon, 9 ribbon roses using the beige silk ribbon, and 1 ribbon rose using the pale pink silk ribbon.

6   Using 3 strands of the green DMC, embroider a heavy calyx onto the base of every rose. Extend a stem from the calyx and join to the fabric, leaving the rose to fall freely. Use the photograph as a guide.

7   Embroider the sprays of French knots and buds using the dusty pink silk ribbon.

8   Using the bronze green silk ribbon, embroider the leaves in leaf stitch.

9   Add calyxes and stems to all the buds and leaves using 3 strands of bronze green DMC.

10   Using the remaining pink silk ribbon, embroider the bow at the top of the silk picture.

11   See pages 159–161 for finishing and making up the cushion.

Finished cushion measures 45 × 38 cm (18 × 15 in). Tracing appears on page 146.

Victorian Oyster Cushion with Pearl Crest

This cushion was inspired by an exhibition of presentation boxes that were made as gifts to royalty, held at the Victoria & Albert Museum in London. Pearls are stitched into a small cameo on a background of grey satin that has been overlaid with pale grey organza, a technique that gives the finished cushion a shimmering effect. Within the pearls are pale pink ribbon roses. The cushion is edged with the same ribbon and finished with a pleated silver satin frill.

EMBROIDERY MATERIALS

30 cm (12 in) square oyster-coloured mesh

1 skein ecru DMC stranded cotton

1 packet small pearls

2 m (2.2 yd) silk ribbon no. 5 (pale pink), 4 mm
  (³⁄₁₆ in) wide

1 m (1.1 yd) pale pink double-sided satin ribbon,
  10 mm (³⁄₈ in) wide

1 porcelain rose cameo

1 skein DMC stranded cotton no. 504
  (pale green)

ASSEMBLY MATERIALS

50 cm (20 in) oyster-coloured pleated mesh

1   Cut out a 22 cm (8½ in) square of mesh.

2   Trace the design onto the fabric in pencil.

3   Using 2 strands of ecru DMC, thread the
pearls into strands and drape according to
the pattern, tacking at intervals.

4   Embroider 4 small and 2 very small roses
in rosette stitch using the pale pink silk
ribbon.

5   Add 4 rosebuds down the centre using the
pale pink satin ribbon in leaf stitch.

6   Using 4 strands of pale green DMC, add
the stems and leaves.

7   Stitch the porcelain rose onto the design
with matching thread.

8   See pages 159–161 for finishing and making
up the cushion.

   Finished cushion measures 20 cm (8 in) square. Tracing appears on page 147.

Bronze Filigree Basket with Poirot Roses Cushion

As a background for this cushion I used pale pink silk with fine gold thread running through it, topped with white tulle. I wanted it to look dainty and feminine, so I made the ribbon roses in different shades of pale pinks and worked the trellis basket using a new technique with gold thread. It's edged with gold braid and finished with a pink silk frill. The subdued lighting, and the gilt finishes on the side table, the chair and the cushion give this setting warmth and character.

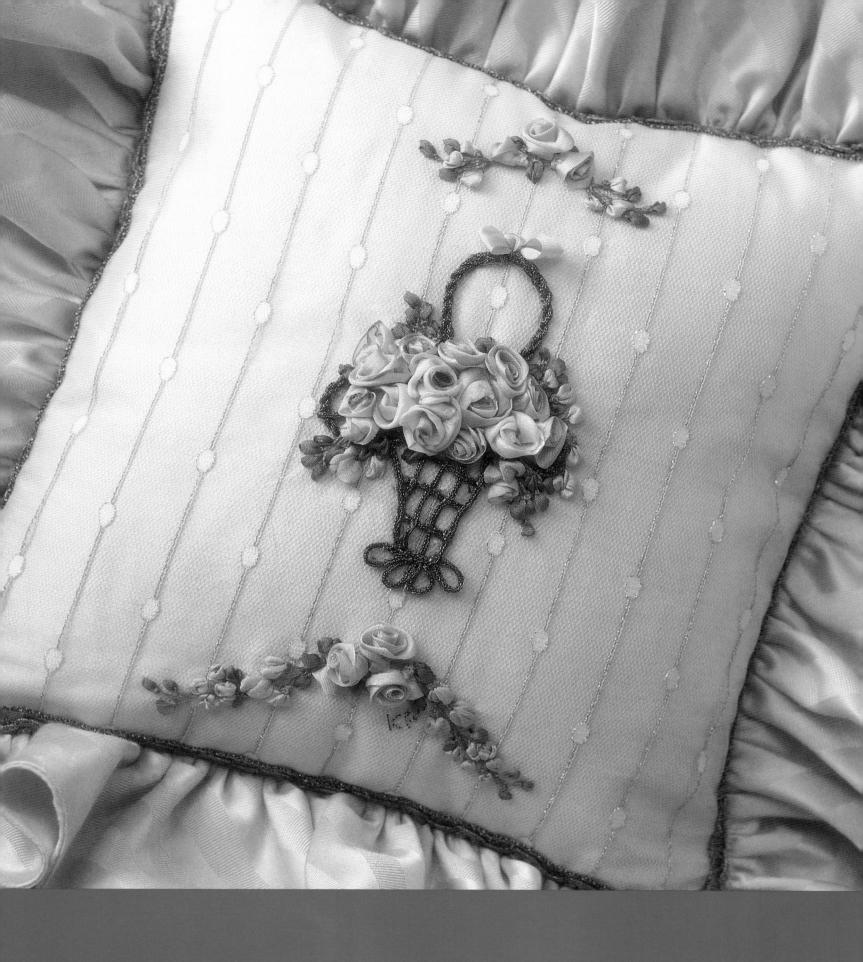

EMBROIDERY MATERIALS

30 cm (12 in) square pale pink dupion silk

30 cm (12 in) square spotted French toile

1 skein DMC stranded cotton no. 543
  (dusty pink)

1 m (1.1 yd) bronze metallic cord

1 skein DMC stranded cotton no. 370
  (bronze green)

2 m (2.2 yd) hand-dyed gold-edged ribbon
  (pale pink), 20 mm (¾ in) wide

3 m (3.3 yd) silk ribbon no. 65 (dusty pink),
  7 mm (½ in) wide

3 m (3.3 yd) silk ribbon no. 65 (dusty pink),
  4 mm (³/₁₆ in) wide

4 m (4.4 yd) silk ribbon no. 143 (bronze green),
  4 mm (³/₁₆ in) wide

ASSEMBLY MATERIALS

1 m (1.1 yd) antique gold braid

pink-and-cream satin striped fabric, cut on
  cross

1   Cut out a 25 cm (10 in) square of dupion silk and toile.

2   Tack the 2 squares of fabric together using a strand of the dusty pink DMC with long running stitch.

3   Trace the design onto the centre of the fabric in pencil.

4   Using the diagram as a guide, lay down the bronze cord in the shape of the basket, tacking with bronze green DMC as you go.

5   Fold the pale pink hand-dyed ribbon in half lengthwise so that both gold edges meet. Use to make 7 ribbon roses of varying sizes.

6   Make 16 ribbon roses of varying sizes using the dusty pink 7 mm-wide silk ribbon.

7   Position all of the roses according to the diagram and stitch down with 2 strands of dusty pink DMC.

8   Using the dusty pink 7 mm-wide silk ribbon, embroider a bow at the top of the basket. Bring the ribbon through the back of the fabric, and up again to form the 2 loops of the bow. Sew over the join of the loops to form a knot.

9   Using the dusty pink 4 mm-wide silk ribbon, embroider the sprays of buds using French knots and leaf stitch.

10 Using the diagram as a guide, embroider the leaves with the bronze green 4 mm-wide silk ribbon.

11 Connect all the leaves to stems using the bronze green DMC.

12 See pages 159–161 for finishing and making up the cushion.

Finished cushion measures 24 cm (9½ in) square. Tracing appears on page 147.

Antique Gold Cushion

The Antique Gold Cushion is set on a wonderful old Louis XVI-style chair from

about the middle of the nineteenth century. Its chipped and battered surface, and its

original Aubusson upholstery, can be read like a book. The cushion was inspired by a

friend who gave me a small piece of very old French tulle in this antique gold colour

with which to make a personal cushion. To the several layers of tulle that make up the

background, I added some braid that has gold metallic thread running through it, the

last piece I had left over from another work. Then I added twists of gold Russia,

which is commonly used to trim lampshades, and embroidered the whole piece with

silk ribbon roses in different shades of pink, setting them off with green ribbon leaves.

The cushion is finished with a gathered tulle edging.

Finished cushion measures 23 × 20 cm (9 × 8 in). Tracing appears on page 147.

EMBROIDERY MATERIALS

1 m (1.1 yd) square gold mesh

25 cm (10 in) ornate brocade ribbon

3 m (3.3 yd) Mokuba bronze metallic ribbon

antique gold thread

1.5 m (1.6 yd) silk ribbon no. 6 (pink),
    7 mm (⅓ in) wide

1 m (1.1 yd) ecru double-sided satin ribbon,
    7 mm (⅓ in) wide

1 m (1.1 yd) Vintage hand-dyed dark pink silk
    ribbon with gold edge, 20 mm (¾ in) wide

1 m (1.1 yd) pink organza ribbon, 7 mm
    (⅓ in) wide

1 m (1.1 yd) pale pink double-sided satin ribbon,
    7 mm (⅓ in) wide

50 cm (20 in) deeper pink double-sided satin
    ribbon, 7 mm (⅓ in) wide

1 m (1.1 yd) Mokuba taffeta ribbon no. 5
    (luminous green), 13 mm (½ in) wide

6 m (6.6 yd) silk ribbon no. 6 (pink),
    4 mm (³⁄₁₆ in) wide

6 m (6.6 yd) silk ribbon no. 56 (antique green),
    4 mm (³⁄₁₆ in) wide

1 skein DMC stranded cotton no. 524 (green)

1   Cut out a piece of gold mesh measuring 25 × 23 cm (10 × 9 in). Tack the piece of brocade ribbon across the middle of the fabric.

2   Trace the design onto the fabric in pencil.

3   Using the bronze metallic ribbon, create the round cornelli design by laying the ribbon flat and tacking down with matching gold thread. To make the centrepiece, form 8 loops of varying sizes and join at the centre. Tack down.

4   Make 9 small ribbon roses using the pink 7 mm-wide silk ribbon. Make 4 small ribbon roses using the ecru double-sided ribbon.

5   Fold the hand-dyed dark pink silk ribbon in half lengthwise so the gold edges meet. Make 6 ribbon roses with the gold edge at the top.

6   Take the left-over piece of pink 7 mm-wide silk ribbon and the pink organza ribbon and place together. Twist the ribbons together and make 4 ribbon roses.

7   Make 4 ribbon roses using the pale pink double-sided satin ribbon. With the deeper pink satin ribbon make 2 small roses.

8   Using the luminous green ribbon make 6 large leaves and 8 very small leaves.

9   Using the photograph as a guide, pin all the roses and leaves onto the fabric. Once you are happy with the way they are sitting, sew each one down securely with 2 strands of matching thread.

10 Embroider the French knots and buds with the pink 4 mm-wide silk ribbon.

11 Add leaves, stems and calyxes using the antique-green silk ribbon.

12 Connect the buds and leaves with 2 strands of the green DMC using French knots and straight stitch.

13 See pages 159–161 for finishing and making up the cushion.

Shimmering
Rose Silk
Cushion

The silk for this shimmering, dreamy cushion came from India. I layered it with a veil of pleated organza and stitched on a silver embroidered panel, into which I worked ribbon roses in contrasting tones. To finish, the panel was edged with silver bullion cord, which was also used to make a simple, but dramatic, frill. The gilt side table holds a multitude of treasures my friend, a keen collector with a good eye, has amassed from her travels. The warm burnished tones of the Louis-style gilt chair provide a lustrous setting for the cushion.

EMBROIDERY MATERIALS

35 cm (14 in) square oyster-coloured pure silk

1 × 25 cm (10 in) hand-embroidered silver panel

50 cm (20 in) pleated silver organza

3 m (3.3 yd) silk ribbon no. 65 (dusty rose pink),
   7 mm (⅓ in) wide

1 m (1.1 yd) silk ribbon no. 3 (white), 7 mm
   (⅓ in) wide

2 m (2.2 yd) silk ribbon no. 13 (pale lemon),
   7 mm (⅓ in) wide

4 m (4.4 yd) silk ribbon no. 5 (pale pink), 7 mm
   (⅓ in) wide

3 m (3.3 yd) silk ribbon no. 101 (pale mauve),
   7 mm (⅓ in) wide

2 m (2.2 yd) silk ribbon no. 90 (pale blue), 7 mm
   (⅓ in) wide

1 reel silver thread

2 m (2.2 yd) silk ribbon no. 71 (chartreuse),
   4 mm (³⁄₁₆ in) wide

3 m (3.3 yd) silk ribbon no. 73 (antique green),
   4 mm (³⁄₁₆ in) wide

1 skein DMC stranded cotton no. 646 (grey
   green)

1 skein DMC stranded cotton no. 524 (pale
   green)

ASSEMBLY MATERIALS

7 m (7.7 yd) silver bullion cord

1   Cut out a piece of silk measuring
    32 × 23 cm (12½ × 9 in).

2   Sew the hand-embroidered silver panel
    down the centre of the silk.

3   Cut out 2 pieces of the pleated organza
    fabric, each measuring 14 × 24 cm
    (5½ × 9½ in) while still pleated. Using the
    diagram as a guide, stitch the fabric down
    either side of the centre panel, making
    sure to keep the pleating gathered.

4   Make 10 ribbon roses using the dusty rose
    pink silk ribbon, 5 in white, 6 in pale lemon,
    13 in pale pink, 2 in pale mauve, and 2 in
    pale blue. Using the photograph as a guide,
    sew the roses into place with 2 strands of
    silver thread.

5   Embroider the sprays of buds in leaf stitch
    and French knots using the rest of the silk
    ribbons. Again, use the photograph as a
    guide for placement.

6   Fill in the greenery by threading 2 strands
    of each green DMC through a needle and
    adding the leaves, calyxes and stems.

7   Edge the centre silver panel with the silver
    bullion cord. Tack down with 2 strands of
    silver thread.

8   See pages 159–161 for finishing and making
    up the cushion.

Finished cushion measures 31 × 21 cm (12 × 8 in). Tracing appears on page 148.

Hanging Basket of Roses

I used the pattern of the fabric to form the shape of the stitching for this piece.

A gold threadwork basket holds a bunch of delicate pink ribbon roses. More roses and buds, worked in ribbon and DMC stranded cotton, are loosely draped over and around the basket, creating an almost musical backdrop.

EMBROIDERY MATERIALS

40 cm (16 in) square patterned brocade

1 small piece antique gold braid

1 reel gold thread

5 m (5.5 yd) silk ribbon no. 6 or 7 (pink),
    7 mm (⅓ in) wide

1 skein DMC stranded cotton no. 3047
    (pale gold)

4 m (4.4 yd) silk ribbon no. 171 (green),
    4 mm (³⁄₁₆ in) wide

1 skein DMC stranded cotton no. 3052
    (green)

1   Cut out a piece of brocade measuring
    25 × 30 cm (10 × 12 in), making sure the
    pattern is centred.

2   Trace the design onto the centre of the
    fabric in pencil.

3   Stitch down the piece of antique gold braid
    to form the body of the basket. Using the
    gold thread, satin stitch the edge of the gold
    braid to create a vase-like shape.

4   Make 14 small ribbon roses using the pink
    silk ribbon.

5   Place 12 of the roses in the basket. Be sure
    to set them quite closely together to create
    a natural look. Stitch them down using a
    strand of the pale gold DMC. Place the other
    2 at the foot of the basket and stitch down.

6   Satin stitch the rope that connects the
    basket to the bow using 4 strands of pale
    gold DMC.

7   Using the pink silk ribbon, embroider the
    other roses using rosette stitch, the buds
    using leaf stitch and the rope using French
    knots.

8   With the remaining pink silk ribbon,
    embroider the bow at the top of the rope.

9   Using the photograph as a guide, embroider
    all of the leaves in leaf stitch with the green
    silk ribbon.

10 Add calyxes and stems using 2 strands of the
    green DMC.

Finished picture measures 15 × 21 cm (6 × 8 in), excluding frame.
Tracing appears on page 148.

Framed
Cream
Organza
Rose
Posy

I love the delicate effect of ribbon roses.

In the Cream Organza Rose Posy, I

countered the all-cream, bridal look by

scattering pink, pale blue and chartreuse

ribbon roses around the outer edge of

the posy. The soft roses are swept

together with a cream taffeta bow and

set against a background of dupion silk.

The pale blue insert and its gold rim lift

the pastels from the posy, and together

with the heavy gilt frame, lend the work

a rich, luxurious feel.

EMBROIDERY MATERIALS

35 cm (14 in) square cream dupion silk

4 m (4.4 yd) Mokuba satin-edged organza
    ribbon no. 12 (cream), 15 mm ($^5/_8$ in) wide

1 m (1.1 yd) silk ribbon no. 65 (dusty pink),
    7 mm ($^1/_3$ in) wide

2 m (2.2 yd) silk ribbon no. 65 (dusty pink),
    4 mm ($^3/_{16}$ in) wide

3 m (3.3 yd) silk ribbon no. 90 (pale blue),
    4 mm ($^3/_{16}$ in) wide

2 m (2.2 yd) silk ribbon no. 156 (cream),
    7 mm ($^1/_3$ in) wide

4 m (4.4 yd) silk ribbon no. 71 (chartreuse),
    4 mm ($^3/_{16}$ in) wide

1 skein DMC stranded cotton no. 472
    (pale lime green)

1 skein DMC stranded cotton no. 3013
    (pale antique green)

25 cm (10 in) cream wired taffeta ribbon

1 skein ecru DMC stranded cotton

1   Cut out a piece of cream dupion silk
measuring 35 cm (14 in) square. Trace the
design onto the centre of the fabric in pencil.

2   Using the cream organza ribbon, make 20
ribbon roses of varying sizes.

3   Pin the first rose in the centre to make the
heart of the bouquet. Position a circle of
roses around the first, leaving the very outer
layer until later.

4   Using the dusty pink 7 mm-wide silk ribbon,
make 3 small ribbon roses and set aside.

5   Using the dusty pink 4 mm-wide silk ribbon,
embroider the sprays of buds using French
knots and leaf stitch.

6   Using the photograph as a guide, fill in the
clusters of blue French knots using the pale
blue silk ribbon.

7   Embroider the large cream buds using the
cream silk ribbon. Use leaf stitch, and finish
with a French knot in the centre.

8   Using the diagram as a guide, embroider the
sprays of ribbon leaves using the chartreuse
silk ribbon.

9   Using a strand of each green DMC, connect
the leaves to the bouquet with calyxes and
stems.

10   Embroider the stems of the posy with the
same threads in long stem stitches.

11   Tie the wired cream taffeta ribbon into a
small bow and secure at the base of the posy
using 2 strands of ecru DMC.

12   Finally, nestle all of the remaining roses
into position and sew down with 2 strands
of matching thread.

Finished picture measures 26 × 28 cm (10 × 11 in), excluding frame.
Tracing appears on page 148.

I AM AN INCURABLE HOARDER OF TEXTILES; I never throw out anything. I have filled boxes with fabric remnants, scraps of braid and odd pieces of ribbon, knowing that one day I will use them. This habit bears fruit when I have a piece of furniture reupholstered. I always gather up the left-over scraps of fabric as they can be used to make up cushions that bring together colours and fabrics in the room.

I love the creative tension between various colours, patterns, styles and shapes, and I love to mix them together whenever and wherever possible. My settings and, of course, my cushions, are a marriage of striped and checked, bold and subdued, patterned and plain. You'll see from the photographs in this book that I have teamed animal prints with floral prints, ribbon roses, tapestries, gingham and even light fabrics such as organza. Success is a matter of trial and error, of training your eye to see the beauty in eclecticism.

I love the creative tension between various colours, patterns, styles and shapes, and I love to mix them together whenever and wherever possible.

I am predictable in my love of faux animal furs and fabrics made to look like animal skins. I bought my first piece of faux fur as a young woman of about eighteen. It was in the style of ocelot skin and I made a three-quarter-length coat from it. Slipping on this garment   >

PAGES 36–37: *This is the living area of a friend. Her couch is covered in leopard print with a rich faux fur throw rug tossed on top. Piles of tapestry cushions and animal prints add to the mix, and a tapestry wall-hanging completes the picture. On a small wine table is my little workbox, made for me by Arnold Eaton, a friend who knows of my love for animal prints.* RIGHT: *This fabulous French commode with its black marble top, intricate inlay work and elaborate drawer-pulls and edging is much loved and treasured. The array of blue-and-white china includes ginger jars, planters, tall urns and boxes, some holding favourite flowers. The timber panelling in the background is actually the back of an old armoire, which I use as a room divider.*

meant instant glamour: I felt like a movie star in it! Since then, my love of animal prints and faux fur has grown and evolved such that today, with a complete disregard for what is fashionable, my wardrobe always includes animal-print scarves in silk, ocelot hosiery, fur cuffs and collars, and at least one faux fur handbag.

In the same way, my home also has an abundance of animal prints. Years ago, I needed some chairs to go with a leather sofa, and after much searching I found a pair of reproduction Louis-style chairs that I had upholstered with tiger-skin fabric. While the leather sofa is long gone, the chairs are still very much a part of my living area, and are now teamed with a lovely down-filled couch covered with a Boyac ocelot print. I find it stimulating that the two fabrics work so well together, and the more I add to them the better they seem to look.

My love of animal prints and faux fur has grown and evolved such that today, with a complete disregard for what is fashionable, my wardrobe always includes animal-print scarves in silk, ocelot hosiery, fur cuffs and collars, and at least one faux fur handbag.

My couch is draped with a faux fur throw rug. I have also draped over one of the chairs another small fur rug that I made from an old coat I'd had for years and had never worn. For that final layered effect, there's my signature touch of cushions of various shapes and sizes. Some of the cushions are made using just the ocelot fabric; others have the ocelot teamed with pieces of petit point and tapestry, scraps of gold braid and even bright floral cotton. The exotic confection of different and unexpected patterns and textiles that can work so well together never ceases to amaze me.

Forget fashion: buy things you love

Ocelot Cushion with Petit Point Insert

For this cushion I combined a small piece of floral petit point with the same ocelot linen that covers my sofa. It has a ruched border of floral chintz, which ties in with the colours of the petit point, and each change of fabric is marked with gold braid. The cushion is in an area of my sitting room that I use all the time. Nearby is a pair of armchairs covered in zebra-skin print that my dogs, Coco and Paris, just love to sit on.

ASSEMBLY MATERIALS

75 cm (29½ in) calico

50 cm (20 in) ocelot fabric

1 × 22 × 18 cm (8½ × 7 in) piece petit point

3 m (3.3 yd) antique gold braid

2 m (2.2 yd) antique gold cord

25 cm (10 in) Sanderson rose-print linen

1 Cut out a 50 × 45 cm (20 × 18 in) piece of calico.

2 Cut out a 35 × 40 cm (14 × 16 in) piece of ocelot and sew onto the calico, making sure that it is evenly placed.

3 Place the petit point on top of the ocelot and sew down. There should be an even border of ocelot around the petit point.

4 Frame the petit point with the antique gold braid and sew into place. Sew the antique gold cord around the inner edge of the frame.

5 Fold the remaining gold cord in half to find the middle. Make a bow and sew onto the upper centre of the design. Using the tails of the bow, measure to each corner and make two more bows. Sew into place. Repeat this step until there are 8 bows around the perimeter of the insert. Trim the bows, and stitch the tails flat to the fabric.

6 Cut out 4 × 7 cm (3 in) strips of the rose-print linen. Sew together with mitred corners to form a square.

7 Gather the inside and outside of the linen and stitch to the ocelot, making sure the mitred corners match the corners of the ocelot and calico.

8 Sew the antique gold braid onto the border of ocelot and linen.

9 See pages 159–161 for finishing and making up the cushion.

Finished cushion measures 50 × 45 cm (20 × 18 in).

I love the freshness of blue-and-white china.

Fuchsia Velvet
Rose Cushion

I used two gauges of gingham, one on top of the other, for this cush-

ion. With a selection of jewel-coloured wools, I embroidered a

massed border of flowers with rayon ribbon roses worked in among

them. The roses that grace the corners are made of velvet ribbons

edged with black, which give the flower petals greater depth. I used

the same ribbon to trim the frill.

EMBROIDERY MATERIALS

1 m (1.1 yd) square black-and-cream tea-dyed cotton, large check

1 m (1.1 yd) square black-and-cream tea-dyed cotton, small check

30 cm (12 in) square calico

1.5 m (1.6 yd) Mokuba rayon ribbon no. 53 (fuchsia), 13 mm (½ in) wide

1.5 m (1.6 yd) Mokuba rayon ribbon no. 28 (red), 13 mm (½ in) wide

1.5 m (1.6 yd) Mokuba rayon ribbon no. 54 (hot pink), 13 mm (½ in) wide

1 skein Paterna yarn no. 610 (green)

1 skein Paterna yarn no. 650 (olive green)

1 skein Paterna yarn no. 311 (purple)

1 skein Paterna yarn no. 340 (jacaranda)

1 skein Paterna yarn no. 710 (gold)

1 skein Paterna yarn no. 351 (hot pink)

1 skein Paterna yarn no. 902 (red)

1 skein Paterna yarn no. 320 (deep purple)

5 m (5.5 yd) Mokuba velvet ribbon no. 54 (fuchsia), 25 mm (1 in) wide

black cotton

1   Cut out a 32 cm (12½ in) square of the large-check fabric. Cut out an 18 cm (7 in) square of the small-check fabric. Tack the small-check fabric onto the centre of the large-check square.

2   Trace the design onto the 30 cm (12 in) square of calico in pencil.

3   Make 6 ribbon roses using the fuchsia rayon ribbon and secure onto the calico.

4   Repeat with the red and hot pink ribbons, using the photograph as a guide.

5   Using the fuchsia rayon ribbon, embroider some buds in leaf stitch on the calico.

6   Fill in the gaps with wool flowers worked in stem and lazy daisy stitches, and bullion knots. Use the photograph to help you with colour placement.

7   Fill in the greenery using stem and leaf stitch.

8   Carefully cut around the wool embroidery, leaving a 5 mm-edge of calico all around.

9   Tack the embroidered pieces around the small-check square to form a frame, making sure you tuck in all the raw edges.

10 Embroider around to blend the edges and to cover any bits of calico that may be showing. French knots and leaf stitch are suitable for this.

11 Make 6 ribbon roses using the fuchsia velvet ribbon. When making the roses, fold the ribbon in half so that the black sides are on the inside and the edges meet at the top of the rose.

12 Position the velvet roses on the corners of the frame and secure with black cotton.

13 See pages 159–161 for finishing and making up the cushion.

Finished cushion measures 30 cm (12 in) square. Tracing appears on page 149.

Mona
Lisa
Cushion

The Mona Lisa print was given to me by a special lady from one of my classes. I set it on a black tea-dyed gingham background, and finished it with black velvet roses and a black bow. The ocelot border and wide black velvet frill highlight the dark tones of this cushion perfectly. The tiger-striped chair, faux wolf throw rug and ocelot lampshade provide little inflections.

EMBROIDERY MATERIALS

40 cm (16 in) square panther cotton

1 m (1.1 yd) square black-and-cream tea-dyed
    cotton, small check

1 Mona Lisa print

2 skeins DMC stranded cotton no. 310 (black)

1.5 m (1.6 yd) Mokuba black velvet ribbon,
    25 mm (1 in) wide

20 cm (8 in) Mokuba black velvet ribbon,
    15 mm ($^5/_8$ in) wide

black cotton

ASSEMBLY MATERIALS

1 m (1.1 yd) square black velvet

1   Cut out a 32 cm (12$^1/_2$ in) square of panther
    fabric. Cut out a piece of check fabric
    measuring 20 × 25 cm (8 × 10 in).

2   Sew the checked fabric onto the centre of
    the panther square. Pipe the edges of the
    checked square with a 25 mm-wide piece of
    black velvet ribbon.

3   Trim the Mona Lisa print into an oval
    measuring 14 cm × 10 cm (5$^1/_2$ × 4 in). Satin
    stitch the print to the middle of the checked
    fabric using all 6 strands of the black DMC.

4   Using the 25 mm-wide velvet ribbon, make
    a small velvet peony rose and 4 ribbon roses.
    Using black cotton, secure the roses at the
    base of the print with small stitches.

5   Make a bow using the 15 mm-wide velvet
    ribbon. Secure into place with the black
    cotton.

6   See pages 159–161 for finishing and making
    up the cushion.

Finished cushion measures 30 cm (12 in) square. Tracing appears on page 150.

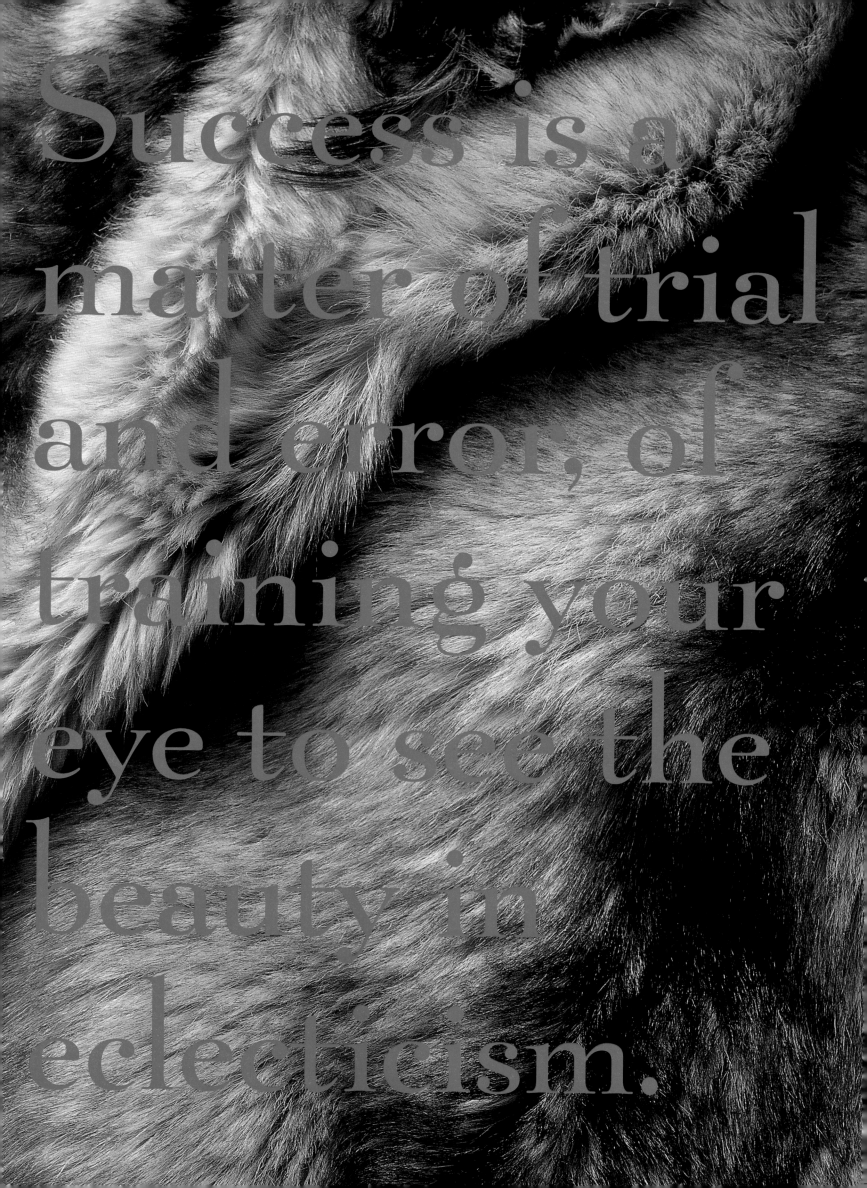

Success is a matter of trial and error, of training your eye to see the beauty in eclecticism.

Polka Dot Posy Cushion

The bright colours of the Polka Dot Posy, gathered together with a little ribbon, are really uplifting. The cushion is quite small, so I added an oversized pleated frill in a yellow polka dot silk that matched the plain yellow fabric. It is complemented by another cushion in the same fabric, wrapped like a gift in ribbons. I made both cushions to brighten up the dull, dun-coloured fabric of this chair.

EMBROIDERY MATERIALS

20 cm (8 in) square yellow dupion silk

2 m (2.2 yd) silk ribbon no. 69 (hot pink), 4 mm ($^3/_{16}$ in) wide

2 m (2.2 yd) silk ribbon no. 117 (blue), 4 mm ($^3/_{16}$ in) wide

2 m (2.2 yd) silk ribbon no. 145 (mid-pink), 4 mm ($^3/_{16}$ in) wide

1 skein DMC stranded cotton no. 307 (yellow)

1 skein DMC stranded cotton no. 3608 (deep pink)

1 skein DMC stranded cotton no. 367 (dark green)

1 skein DMC stranded cotton no. 3053 (pale green)

50 cm (20 in) silk ribbon no. 56 (antique green), 4 mm ($^3/_{16}$ in) wide

ASSEMBLY MATERIALS

1 m (1.1 yd) hot pink double-sided satin ribbon, 25 mm (1 in) wide

1.5 m (1.6 yd) pleated polka dot ribbon (or matching pleated silk)

1   Cut out a 17 cm (6½ in) square of dupion silk.

2   Trace the design onto the centre of the fabric in pencil.

3   Using the hot pink silk ribbon, embroider 2 roses using rosette stitch. With the same ribbon fill in the buds with leaf stitch and French knots. Use the diagram as a guide to placement.

4   With the blue silk ribbon, embroider a rose in rosette stitch and the buds in leaf stitch.

5   Embroider the remaining flowers and buds in the mid-pink silk ribbon.

6   Using all 6 strands of the yellow DMC, embroider a French knot in the centre of the 2 rosette-stitch roses and a small bud.

7   Embroider a spray of French knots in deep pink DMC.

8   Using the photograph as a guide, add the stems and leaves using 2 strands of each green DMC. (This gives a variegated effect.)

9   With the antique-green silk ribbon, tie a bow at the base of the posy and anchor it into place with matching cotton.

10   See pages 159–161 for finishing and making up the cushion.

Finished cushion measures 15 cm (6 in) square. Tracing appears on page 150.

Pink Florentine Cushion

My dear friend Sue Dickens made this stunning Florentine silk brocade cushion especially for this book. The silk insert was aged for an antique effect and sewn onto the brocade. It was then framed with Madeira cord and fine gold thread loops and twirls at the head and foot. Sue is a very talented passementerie artist, and could not resist making baby thistles, a medallion and some velvety pompoms to embellish this sumptuous cushion.

EMBROIDERY MATERIALS

1 × 20 × 15 cm (8 × 6 in) aged satin picture
(see page 173 for instructions on how to age
satin picture)

50 cm (20 in) Florentine brocade

1 m (1.1 yd) McDougall's gold cord no. 11552

1 reel Madeira thread no. 40 (gold)

1 reel Madeira metallic thread no. 5012 (gold)

1 skein Appeltons crewel wool no. 10 (rose red)

1 egg-shaped piece of pellon 2 × 3 cm (³⁄₄ × 1¹⁄₄ in)

1   Place the satin picture in the centre of the
    Florentine brocade and tack down. Machine
    sew along the edge of the picture.

2   Sew down the gold cord around the edge of
    the picture with the Madeira gold thread,
    taking care to cover the machine line.
    Arrange the ends as in the picture and sew
    down securely onto the fabric to prevent the
    ends unravelling.

3   Using the photograph as a guide, and
    beginning from the centre outwards, make
    the fine gold loops and leaf embellishments
    with the Madeira metallic thread on the
    bottom part of the frame. Couch into place
    as you go along using the gold thread. It is
    easier to make a symmetrical pattern if you
    use 4 needles and work both sides at the
    same time. Repeat for the top of the frame,
    again using the photograph as a guide.

Finished cushion measures 38 × 42 cm (15 × 16¹⁄₂ in). Tracing appears on page 150.

4   To make the bottom thistles, fold a skein of Appeltons wool in half. Cut into quarters. Fold each quarter in half again and tie a holding thread tightly on the fold. Wrap thread firmly around opposite end 6 times to make a secure binding. With a pair of sharp scissors, trim close to the binding. Repeat for the other thistles.

5   The thistles are couched with a detached buttonhole stitch with a twist, which is a traditional method of making mesh covering. Start by working a row of approximately 8 loose blanket stitches around the band of thread at the cut end of the thistle.

6   Work the second row by inserting the needle through the loop formed, winding the thread in an anti-clockwise direction around the point of the needle. Place thumb lightly over the needle and pull the thread through gently. Ease the knot so that it sits in the middle of the loop. Pin this loop in place and repeat to form more stitches, pinning each stitch to complete the circle. As you work,

remove the pin in front of the newly formed loop so you always work with 6 or 7 pins.

7   Work more rows in this manner until the head of the thistle is completely covered. Fasten off by sewing the stitches tightly together at the top of the thistle. Place the thistles according to the photograph and sew down with fine gold thread.

8   To make the medallion, tack the egg-shaped pellon into position. Cover the top with Appeltons crewel wool that has been couched in places with seed couching. Outline the medallion by couching fine gold cord to frame it.

9   Two edges of the cushion have been trimmed with multiple pompoms on a cord, clipped to give them a velvety finish. I suggest you see Susan Dickens's *The Art of Tassel Making* for details on how to make them.

10 See pages 159–161 for finishing and making up the cushion.

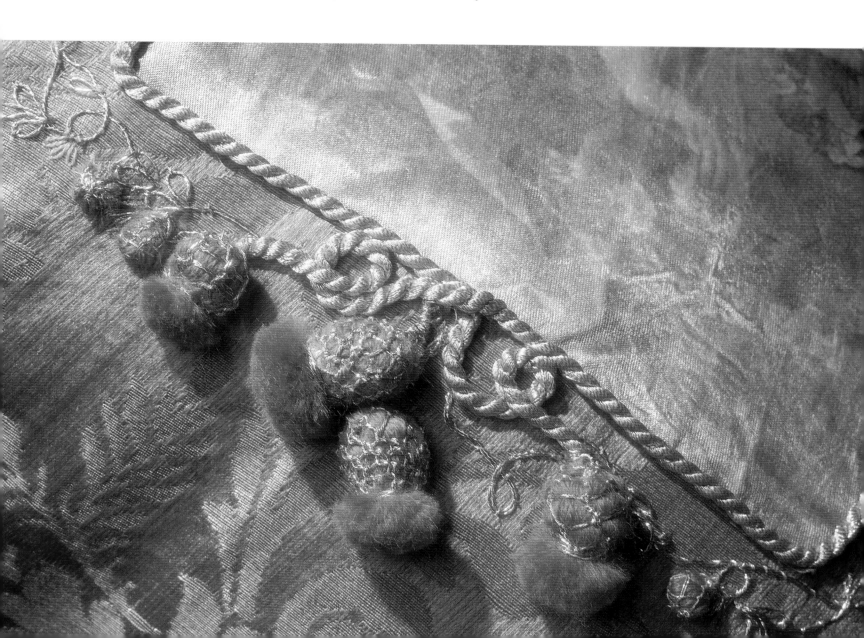

Odenile
Striped
Cushion

The delicate proportions of the Odenile Striped Cushion are well suited to this lavish setting, which comprises a much-loved Louis saloon chair, a French Louis screen and a gilt side table holding a magnificent composition of antique crystal *objets d'art*. The cushion was designed around the ruching, which I laid out in a lattice pattern on the striped dupion silk. A sprinkling of pale grey and pink roses and bows was added, and it was finished with a pleated frill.

EMBROIDERY MATERIALS

30 cm (12 in) square striped dupion silk

10 m (11 yd) Mokuba grey cotton gauze ribbon, 8 mm (³⁄₁₀ in) wide

1 skein DMC stranded cotton no. 762 (pale grey)

2 m (2.2 yd) silver double-sided satin ribbon, 10 mm (³⁄₈ in) wide

2 m (2.2 yd) silk ribbon no. 7 (pink), 7 mm (¹⁄₃ in) wide

1 skein DMC stranded cotton no. 819 (pale pink)

1 m (1.1 yd) silk ribbon no. 73 (antique green), 7 mm (¹⁄₃ in) wide

1 skein DMC stranded cotton no. 524 (pale green)

ASSEMBLY MATERIALS

50 cm (20 in) pleated matching silk

1   Cut out an oval piece of silk measuring 27 × 22 cm (10½ × 8½ in).

2   Trace the design onto the fabric in pencil, taking care to centre it.

3   Take a metre of the grey gauze ribbon and do a gathering stitch down the centre using a strand of pale grey DMC. Gather and place onto the design. Stitch down at intervals using a strand of pale grey DMC. Repeat until you have completed the lattice and oval design.

4   Use the remaining grey gauze ribbon to embroider the 2 ribbon bows without tails.

5   Make 10 ribbon roses using the silver double-sided satin ribbon. Secure into place using 2 strands of pale grey DMC.

6   Make 7 ribbon roses using the pink silk ribbon. Secure into place with a strand of pale pink DMC.

7   Using the pink silk ribbon, embroider the sprays of buds in leaf stitch.

8   Embroider the leaves either side of the silver roses using the antique-green silk ribbon.

9   Add calyxes and stems using 3 strands of pale green DMC.

10 See pages 159–161 for finishing and making up the cushion.

Finished cushion measures 25 × 20 cm (10 × 8 in). Tracing appears on page 151.

Silver Posy Cushion

This pomander-shaped posy is enhanced by its set-

ting of silver-topped cut-glass bottles, some of

which still carry a trace of scent. The intricacy of

the ribbon roses worked on the striped dupion silk

seems to be echoed in the well-wrought planes and

grooves of the bottles. In order to create the effect

of a bas-relief, the bows and loops were left rather

loose and tactile. To finish, the cushion was embel-

lished with a frill that had been cut on the cross.

The three main colours of the flowers were picked

up on the frill for a luscious finish.

EMBROIDERY MATERIALS

20 cm (8 in) square antique-green-and-white
silk

3 m (3.3 yd) silk ribbon no. 101 (mauve), 7 mm
(⅓ in) wide

3 m (3.3 yd) silk ribbon no. 22 (fuchsia), 7 mm
(⅓ in) wide

3 m (3.3 yd) silk ribbon no. 56 (olive green),
7 mm (⅓ in) wide

3 m (3.3 yd) silk ribbon no. 73 (antique green),
4 mm (³⁄₁₆ in) wide

1 skein DMC stranded cotton no. 3743 (dusty
mauve)

1 skein DMC stranded cotton no. 524 (antique
green)

ASSEMBLY MATERIALS

50 cm (20 in) antique-green silk

1 Cut out a piece of silk measuring 20 cm
(8 in) square.

2 Trace the design onto the centre of the
fabric in pencil.

3 Make 2 ribbon roses using the mauve silk
ribbon, 3 with the fuchsia ribbon, and
3 with the olive green ribbon.

4 Thread the mauve ribbon through a needle
and embroider 2 roses in the posy in rosette
stitch. Use the photograph as a guide.

5 Again using the photograph as a guide,
embroider sprays of ribbon buds in leaf
stitch using the antique-green ribbon.
Repeat with the fuchsia, mauve and olive
green ribbons.

6 Embroider the clusters of French knots
using all 6 strands of the dusty mauve DMC.

7 Fill in the greenery using 3 strands of the
antique-green DMC. Use calyx, straight
and leaf stitch for the posy, and long
straight stitches for the stems.

8 Using the antique-green ribbon, embroider
the double bow above the posy using the
ribbon bow instructions. Extend and twist
the tails and finish by bringing through the
back of the fabric. Fasten off.

9 Embroider a double bow at the base of
the posy. Extend and twist the tails to the
bottom corners. Bring them through to
the back of the fabric and fasten off.

10 Using the photograph as a guide, make a
small posy of French knots with the ribbons
and dusty mauve DMC in the centre of the
top bow. Do the same for the 2 posies at
the tails of the lower bow.

11 Fill in the greenery in the posies using
3 strands of the green DMC.

12 See pages 159–161 for finishing and making
up the cushion.

Finished cushion measures 18 cm (7 in) square. Tracing appears on page 151.

I AM SIMPLY PASSIONATE ABOUT FLOWERS and, not surprisingly, most of my work is centred on their splendour. No matter where I go or what I am doing, whether I am walking through a garden, browsing in a shop, or leafing through magazines, I am always aware of the flowers around me and wondering how I can translate them into a piece of embroidery. For me, flowers are a symbol of joy, celebration, generosity and romance. They are also a constant reminder of the changing seasons, and of the passing of time.

I like to be surrounded by flowers in my home – not only vases of cut flowers, but also floral upholstery fabrics, paintings and still-life pictures, my collection of greeting cards and postcards, and the floral dinnerware that I use every day. Again, many of the pieces are second-hand and have been gathered over the years – a cup here, a saucer there. Nothing quite matches, but when put together, the array of blooms creates a sumptuous effect that is quite a fitting tribute to mother nature herself!

> *I am always aware of the flowers around me and wondering how I can translate them into a piece of embroidery.*

Many people seem to be afraid of using strong colours when decorating, but a temporary lift can be obtained easily by adding a few vases of brightly coloured flowers to a room. Everyone has their favourite flower. My mother's was the violet. Personally, I best love spring flowers for their vibrant colours. Loose arrangements of daffodils, tulips, hyacinths and irises that look as though they have   >

PAGES 72–73: *I often sit and work at my dining table, which is draped with a colourful Russian shawl embroidered with floral motifs. Inspiration is all around me – the flowers in the vase, the lovely floral teacup, the design books.*

For me, flowers are a symbol of joy, celebration, generosity and romance.

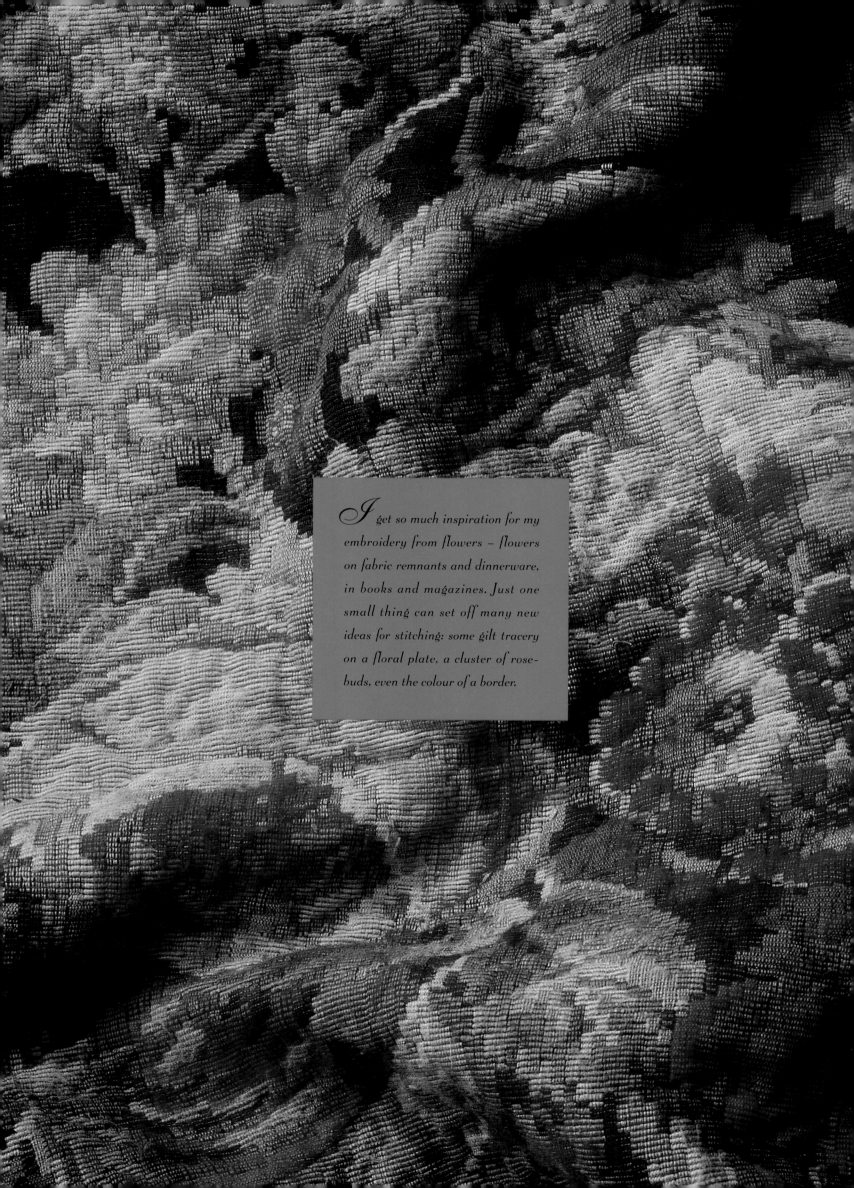

I get so much inspiration for my embroidery from flowers – flowers on fabric remnants and dinnerware, in books and magazines. Just one small thing can set off many new ideas for stitching: some gilt tracery on a floral plate, a cluster of rose-buds, even the colour of a border.

just been gathered from the garden never fail to cheer and uplift me. I also love the fragility and femininity of roses. Imagine a vase full of blooms of just one colour: a mix of roses and stocks or tulips for a white-on-white look, or sweet peas and pink roses for a study in pink. With the wonderful variety of flowers available, it would be impossible not to brighten up a favourite nook!

Everyone has their favourite flower. My mother's was the violet. I best love spring flowers for their vibrant colours.

I must admit that quite often I don't have any fresh flowers in my home at all. Instead, I use artificial flowers made of silk. I know many people reel back in horror at the very mention of fake flowers, but I think you either love them or hate them. Artificial flowers have been used as decoration for centuries, and some display true quality, beauty and real skill. Each silken leaf and petal is hand-crafted and hand-finished, and more often than not you have to look very closely to realise that they are, in fact, made of silk. I am particularly fond of the fake forced bulbs I have placed in blue-and-white ginger jars.

Try mixing fresh flowers with an arrangement of silk ones and see if your friends can pick the difference. Artificial flowers are not cheap, but in the long run they are less expensive, as replenishing cut flowers every week can prove costly. And as with buying anything, my advice is always to select the very best quality you can afford. Be generous with your flowers, whether they are real or fake.

LEFT: *These delicate sweet peas and pink and white roses arranged in my mother's vase make a pretty picture. They are complemented by the potpourri of dried rosebuds which have been placed in a small vegetable dish – an example of how items can be used for purposes for which they were not designed! Overseeing this setting of pink serenity is a bronze boy that I bought at an auction because of his lovely cherubic face.*

French Blue Velvet
Rose Cushion
and
Matching French
Blue Cushion

I love the simplicity of gingham. I often use tea-dyed gingham, which gives a slightly worn look. These cushions are made from two gauges of deep French blue gingham; a large-check square on top of a small-check square, and vice versa. The combination of gingham, bows, blue velvet ribbon roses and brightly coloured spring flowers oozes rustic informality, which I find very appealing. I can imagine these cushions being

used to soften the hard seats of a French bistro setting on an outdoor terrace or a balcony, or to add a touch of the country to a family room.

French Blue Velvet Rose Cushion

EMBROIDERY MATERIALS

1 m (1.1 yd) square blue-and-cream tea-dyed cotton, small check

1 m (1.1 yd) square blue-and-cream tea-dyed cotton, large check

2 skeins Paterna yarn no. 570 (navy)

2.5 m (2.7 yd) Mokuba velvet ribbon no. 20 (blue), 15 mm (⅝ in) wide

1 m (1.1 yd) Mokuba rayon ribbon no. 53 (fuchsia), 13 mm (½ in) wide

1 m (1.1 yd) Mokuba rayon ribbon no. 26 (blue), 13 mm (½ in) wide

1 m (1.1 yd) Mokuba rayon ribbon no. 54 (hot pink), 13 mm (½ in) wide

1 skein Paterna yarn no. 651 (green)

1 skein Paterna yarn no. 690 (green)

1 skein Paterna yarn no. 710 (gold)

1 skein Paterna yarn no. 340 (jacaranda)

1 skein Paterna yarn no. 351 (fuchsia)

1 skein Paterna yarn no. 354 (pink)

1 skein Paterna yarn no. 972 (bright red)

1 skein Paterna yarn no. 311 (purple)

matching cotton

ASSEMBLY MATERIALS

3.5 m (3.8 yd) Mokuba velvet ribbon no. 20 (blue), 25 mm (1 in) wide

1   Cut out a 32 cm (12½ in) square of the small-check fabric. Cut out a 15 cm (6 in) square of the large-check fabric. Tack the large-check square onto the centre of the small-check square.

2   Trace the design onto the fabric in pencil.

3   Satin stitch the bows using one strand of navy wool.

4   Make 8 ribbon roses using the blue velvet ribbon. Position them onto the fabric and secure with matching cotton.

5   With the fuchsia rayon ribbon, make 3 ribbon roses and secure onto the fabric, using the photograph as a guide. Add 2 buds using leaf stitch.

6   Make 2 ribbon roses with the blue rayon ribbon and secure onto the fabric. Add 2 buds using leaf stitch.

7   Using the hot pink rayon ribbon, embroider 7 buds in leaf stitch.

8   Fill in the wool flowers using bullion and French knots and straight stitch. Use the photograph as a guide to colour and placement.

9   Fill in the greenery using stem and leaf stitches.

10 See pages 159–161 for finishing and making up the cushion.

Finished cushion measures 28 cm (11 in) square. Tracing appears on page 152.

Matching French Blue Cushion

EMBROIDERY MATERIALS

1 m (1.1 yd) square blue-and-cream tea-dyed
   cotton, large check

1 m (1.1 yd) square blue-and-cream tea-dyed
   cotton, small check

2 skeins Paterna yarn no. 570 (navy)

1 m (1.1 yd) Mokuba rayon ribbon no. 53
   (fuchsia), 13 mm (½ in) wide

1 m (1.1 yd) Mokuba rayon ribbon no. 26 (blue),
   13 mm (½ in) wide

1 m (1.1 yd) Mokuba rayon ribbon no. 54
   (hot pink), 13 mm (½ in) wide

1 skein Paterna yarn no. 642 (green)

1 skein Paterna yarn no. 690 (green)

1 skein Paterna yarn no. 710 (gold)

1 skein Paterna yarn no. 320 (purple)

1 skein Paterna yarn no. 340 (jacaranda)

1 skein Paterna yarn no. 972 (red)

1 skein Paterna yarn no. 354 (pink)

1 skein Paterna yarn no. D511 (green-gold)

matching cotton

ASSEMBLY MATERIALS

8 m (8.8 yd) navy blue double-sided satin
   ribbon, 10 mm (³⁄₈ in) wide

1   Cut out a 32 cm (12½ in) square of the
    large-check fabric. Cut out a 15 cm (6 in)
    square of the small-check fabric. Tack the
    small-check square onto the centre of the
    large-check square.

2   Trace the design onto the fabric in pencil.

3   Satin stitch the bows using one strand of
    navy wool.

4   Using the fuchsia rayon ribbon, make
    4 ribbon roses and sew into place with
    matching cotton. Add 9 buds in leaf stitch
    with the same ribbon.

5   With the blue rayon ribbon, make 4 ribbon
    roses and secure onto the fabric.

6   Make 4 ribbon roses with the hot pink
    rayon ribbon and secure into position.
    Add 1 bud and 12 French knots with the
    same ribbon as indicated in the diagram.

7   Using the photograph as a guide, fill in the
    wool flowers with bullion and French knots,
    and lazy daisy and rosette stitches.

8   Fill in the greenery using stem and leaf
    stitches.

9   See pages 159–161 for finishing and making
    up the cushion.

Finished cushion measures 28 cm (11 in) square. Tracing appears on page 152.

Julia's Rose Cushion

I was inspired to make this cushion

because of a rose called Julia that was

given to me by my mother's oldest

friend. I chose a pink self-striped silk as

the background because the colour of the

fabric blended so well with the colour of

the ribbons used for the roses. The new

rose that I created for this cushion uses

organza and dentil-edged ribbons to

stunning effect.

1 m (1.1 yd) square pink-striped satin

2.5 m (2.7 yd) Mokuba scallop-edged taffeta
    ribbon no. 40 (dusty pink), 40 mm
    (1½ in) wide

2.5 m (2.7 yd) Mokuba satin-edged organza
    ribbon no. 29 (dusty pink), 25 mm
    (1 in) wide

2 m (2.2 yd) Mokuba rayon ribbon no. 10
    (silver), 13 mm (½ in) wide

1 m (1.1 yd) Mokuba rayon ribbon no. 18
    (green), 13 mm (½ in) wide

1 skein DMC stranded cotton no. 646
    (green-grey)

matching cotton

1   Cut out a 28 cm (11 in) square of satin.

2   Cut a 25 cm (10 in) strip of each dusty pink
    ribbon and place the wrong sides together.
    Make the new rose according to the
    instructions on page 166. To make the outer
    petals, alternate the organza ribbon with
    the taffeta ribbon.

3   Sew the 2 large roses back-to-back in the
    centre of the cushion with matching cotton.

4   Using the diagram as a guide, loosely drape
    and curl the silver rayon ribbon around the
    roses to create a background of bows.
    Anchor the bows at regular intervals.

5   Using both the remaining dusty pink ribbons
    together, make 4 large rosebuds. Secure onto
    the fabric with matching cotton.

6   With a chenille needle, embroider the green
    leaves and calyxes using the green rayon
    ribbon.

7   Using all 6 strands of the green-grey DMC,
    connect the leaves and buds to the centre
    roses using French knots and straight
    stitches.

8   See pages 159–161 for finishing and making
    up the cushion.

Finished cushion measures 25 cm (10 in) square. Tracing appears on page 153.

Antique Velvet Garland Cushion

The Louis tub chair in this reading nook is the ideal place for some lovely cushions. The inspiration for this particular cushion came from a bunch of velvet violets that used to belong to my mother. I separated the bunch and placed the violets individually in a circle, then added ribbon roses in muted shades of pink and beige. The cushion is worked in beige silk with a pleated frill that is from a slightly different dye lot to give it a somewhat aged look.

EMBROIDERY MATERIALS

30 cm (12 in) square ecru dupion silk

6 antique velvet violets

1.5 m (1.6 yd) ecru double-sided ribbon, 7 mm
  ($\frac{1}{3}$ in) wide

1.5 m (1.6 yd) Mokuba rayon ribbon no. 12
  (cream), 13 mm ($\frac{1}{2}$ in) wide

1.5 m (1.6 yd) silk ribbon no. 65 (dusty pink),
  7 mm ($\frac{1}{3}$ in) wide

1 skein ecru DMC stranded cotton

2 m (2.2 yd) silk ribbon no. 56 (antique green),
  4 mm ($\frac{3}{16}$ in) wide

1 skein DMC stranded cotton no. 732 (green)

ASSEMBLY MATERIALS

20 cm (8 in) square matching pleated silk

1   Cut out a 22 cm ($8\frac{1}{2}$ in) square of dupion
    silk.

2   Trace the design onto the fabric in pencil.
    Pin on the 6 antique violets in a circle.

3   Using the ecru double-sided ribbon, make 7
    ribbon roses of varying sizes. Make 6 ribbon
    roses in the cream rayon ribbon and 7 roses
    in the dusty pink silk ribbon.

4   Position your ribbon roses around the
    violets to create a garland of flowers.
    Cluster the roses close together to create a
    natural look. Pin each rose in place. When
    you are satisfied with the way the flowers
    sit, sew down each flower with one strand
    of ecru DMC.

5   Using the antique-green silk ribbon,
    embroider the foliage in leaf stitch.

6   With 4 strands of the green DMC, connect
    the leaves to the base of the flowers using
    French knots and stem stitch.

7   See pages 159–161 for finishing and making
    up the cushion.

Finished cushion measures 20 cm (8 in) square. Tracing appears on page 153.

daffodils tulips hyacinths

magnolias jasmine orchids roses violets sweet peas lavender jon

poppies

Ivana Trump Cushion

The silk background of the Ivana Trump Cushion provides a good contrast both to

the textured fabric of this small Louis-style couch and the tactile weave of the sur-

rounding tapestries. I wove a circular trellis with old satin ribbons that came from a

lingerie factory. Roses of all sizes – made from different types of ribbon and in vary-

ing shades of pink – show flowers in various stages of bloom. The cushion is edged

with a pale green velvet ribbon.

EMBROIDERY MATERIALS

40 cm (16 in) pale blue dupion silk

2 m (2.2 yd) pale pink double-sided satin
ribbon, 10 mm (3/8 in) wide

1 skein DMC stranded cotton no. 819
(pale pink)

3 m (3.3 yd) Mokuba satin-edged organza
ribbon no. 31 (pale pink), 25 mm (1 in) wide

2 m (2.2 yd) Mokuba satin-edged organza
ribbon no. 31 (pale pink), 15 mm (5/8 in) wide

1.5 m (1.6 yd) pale pink double-sided satin
ribbon, 15 mm (5/8 in) wide

4 m (4.4 yd) Mokuba rayon ribbon no. 31
(pale pink), 13 mm (1/2 in) wide

4 m (4.4 yd) silk ribbon no. 71 (chartreuse),
4 mm (3/16 in) wide

1 skein DMC stranded cotton no. 472
(chartreuse)

1 skein DMC stranded cotton no. 3012
(antique green)

1 skein DMC stranded cotton no. 3013
(pale antique green)

1 m (1.1 yd) wired taffeta ribbon (pale blue),
15 mm (5/8 in) wide

1 Cut out a piece of silk measuring 37 cm
   (14 1/2 in) square.

2 Trace the design onto the centre of the
   fabric in pencil.

3 Lay down the ribbon trellis using the pale
   pink 10 mm-wide double-sided satin ribbon
   and tack down with 2 strands of pale pink
   DMC.

4 Using the pale pink 25 mm-wide satin-
   edged organza ribbon, make 4 peony roses.

5 Make the centres of 4 peony roses with the
   pale pink 25 mm-wide satin-edged organza
   ribbon folded in half lengthwise. Use the
   pale pink 15 mm-wide satin-edged organza
   ribbon for the outer petals.

6 Make 6 ribbon roses using the pale pink
   15 mm-wide satin-edged organza ribbon.

7 Make 4 ribbon roses and 5 buds using the
   pale pink 15 mm-wide double-sided satin
   ribbon.

8 Make 18 ribbon roses of varying sizes using
   the pale pink rayon ribbon. Use the smaller
   roses as the buds.

9 Position all of the roses onto the fabric and
   secure with 2 strands of pale pink DMC.
   Place the rayon ribbon buds on their sides
   for a more natural look.

10 Using the pink rayon ribbon, embroider
   the buds in leaf stitch.

11 Embroider the leaves using the chartreuse
   silk ribbon.

12 Thread 2 strands of each green DMC
   through a needle and embroider calyxes and
   stems on the base of each rose, bud and leaf.

13 Cut the pale blue wired taffeta ribbon into
   2 × 50 cm (20 in) lengths and tie 2 bows.
   Secure in place with 2 strands of green
   DMC. Use the photograph as a guide.

14 See pages 159–161 for finishing and making
   up the cushion.

Finished cushion measures 35 cm (14 in) square. Tracing appears on page 154.

Surrounded with flowers.

Cream Carnation Posy Cushion

The Cream Carnation Posy reveals a new flower I have devised,

which uses ribbon edges to resemble a carnation. Lots of roses and

buds made of the same cream ribbon, some with fine gold stamens,

add to the lushness of this cream-on-cream arrangement. The cush-

ion is edged with gold braid and finished with a pleated frill.

EMBROIDERY MATERIALS

30 cm (12 in) square cream dupion silk

9 m (9.9 yd) cream double-sided satin ribbon, 10 mm (³⁄₈ in) wide

2 m (2.2 yd) Mokuba satin-edged organza ribbon no. 12 (cream), 15 mm (⁵⁄₈ in) wide

1 skein ecru DMC stranded cotton

4 m (4.4 yd) silk ribbon no. 156 (cream), 4 mm (³⁄₁₆ in) wide

1 skein DMC stranded cotton no. 372 (green-gold)

1 skein DMC stranded cotton no. 3046 (gold)

gold thread

1 m (1.1 yd) silk ribbon no. 156 (cream), 7 mm (¹⁄₃ in) wide

ASSEMBLY MATERIALS

50 cm (20 in) oyster-coloured pleated frill

30 cm (12 in) gold braid, threaded with cream satin ribbon

1   Cut out a piece of dupion silk measuring 28 × 26 cm (11 × 10 in).

2   Trace the design onto the fabric in pencil.

3   Using the cream double-sided satin ribbon, make 8 ribbon carnations.

4   Fold the cream satin-edged organza ribbon in half and make 12 small ribbon roses.

5   Secure all the carnations and roses into place with ecru DMC.

6   Using the cream 4 mm-wide silk ribbon, embroider the French knots and buds.

7   Thread a strand of green-gold DMC and a strand of gold DMC through a needle and fill in all the stems and leaves.

8   Add a few French knots in gold thread as highlights.

9   Using the cream 7 mm-wide silk ribbon, embroider 2 bows at the base of the bunches of carnations. Take the ribbon through from the back of the fabric, form 2 loops, and cover the join with a small straight stitch to act as the knot.

10 See pages 159–161 for finishing and making up the cushion.

Finished cushion measures 22 cm (8½ in) square. Tracing appears on page 154.

Ribbons and Bows Cushion

The roses on this cushion are accentuated by a medley of rose-sprinkled patterns, from real blooms in the vase to those on the Limoges box and the hand-painted furniture. The cushion was inspired by a small piece of flowery cotton I found in my sewing box. I placed the panel onto the middle of a piece of plain damask and traced out the pattern, which I worked with twirled ribbon and ribbon roses. The finished cushion has been given a generous pleated calico frill and edged with pre-war satin ribbons. The frill seems to mirror the curvy lip of the cherub dish – a happy accident!

EMBROIDERY MATERIALS

25 cm (10 in) blue-and-white striped silk

2 m (2.2 yd) silk ribbon no. 90 (pale blue), 7 mm ($\frac{1}{3}$ in) wide

2.5 m (2.3 yd) silk ribbon no. 73 (antique blue), 4 mm ($\frac{3}{16}$ in) wide

1 m (1.1 yd) silk ribbon no. 53 (old gold), 4 mm ($\frac{3}{16}$ in) wide

1 skein DMC stranded cotton no. 927 (antique blue)

1 skein DMC stranded cotton no. 524 (sage green)

ASSEMBLY MATERIALS

20 cm (8 in) antique-green pleated silk

50 cm (20 in) blue scallop-edged ribbon

1 Cut out a 24 × 20 cm (9½ × 8 in) piece of silk.

2 Trace the design onto the centre of the fabric in pencil.

3 Using the pale blue silk ribbon, make 3 medium-sized ribbon roses and 2 tiny roses.

4 With the remaining pale blue ribbon, embroider the sprays of buds in leaf stitch.

5 Using the antique-blue silk ribbon, embroider the other buds in leaf stitch. Take care to leave a gap between the petals. Embroider a French knot using the old gold silk ribbon in those spaces.

6 Using all 6 strands of the antique-blue DMC and the photograph as a guide, embroider clusters of French knots.

7 Fill in the greenery using 2 strands of the sage green DMC. Connect all the buds and French knots to the stems with a calyx stitch.

8 Embroider a bow at the base of the posy with the remaining antique-blue silk ribbon.

9 See pages 159–161 for finishing and making up the cushion.

Finished cushion measures 22 × 18 cm (8½ × 7 in). Tracing appears on page 156.

WHEN I WAS MUCH YOUNGER, my favourite auction house was owned by an elderly and very grumpy man who, strangely enough, had a white porcelain cherub hanging over his desk. I loved that cherub and desperately wanted it, but he refused to sell it to me because, he said, 'it keeps me honest'. Since then, playful cherubs have become a feature of my decorating style. I believe they are the angels of love, epitomising the things I treasure most of all – and which, sadly, I think are all too rare in our lives – romance and love.

Amidst all the things in my home there is always a place for my cherubs, who have somehow found their way into every room!

Within my little home I have tried to create a delightful haven, and to fill it with beautiful objects and gorgeous fabrics that invite you to touch, to hold, to feel, or simply to feast your eyes on. Amidst all these things there is always a place for my impish cherubs, who have somehow found their way into every room! There are statues of angelic cherubs on tables and consoles; cherub vases holding freshly gathered flowers; cherubs framed in pictures; cherubs in fabrics and books; and even two Capodimonte cherubs that watch over me from above my bed as I sleep. I am quite sure that cherubs bring good luck and that they shield their owners from harm.

PAGES 110–111: *This small table was hand-painted by Lisa Moran, a very talented decorative artist. On it is an old letter rack that belonged to my father. It is filled with my favourite cards – all sent to me by Lisa or my daughter, Charlotte. Scattered across the front are some old sewing pieces I've collected – a silver thimble, a needle case, a pin dish and a pin cushion, as well as framed photos of my children.* LEFT: *This dainty antique French commode side table was once a stained-brown colour. I asked Jane Devine, an artist friend, to paint it to match the tall porcelain statue I had bought for my mother. Surrounding this centrepiece is a collection of my favourite porcelain pieces and, of course, a vase of fresh blooms.*

It doesn't matter what colour you choose as long as it's one you'll love waking up to.

Cherubs with Grapes Cushion

Nestled in a cloud of white silk, this cushion is truly angelic. I combined a little cherub, hand-painted by Lisa Moran, with some lovely French chenille fringe braid in pink, blue and cream, on a background of off-white silk. The cherub is decorated with garlands of silken flowers, their colours specially chosen to match the colours of the braid. Above each wing is a cluster of pearly grapes.

EMBROIDERY MATERIALS

25 cm (10 in) square cream dupion silk

1 hand-painted cherub

1 skein ecru DMC stranded cotton

2 m (2.2 yd) pale pink double-sided satin
ribbon, 7 mm (⅓ in) wide

3 m (3.3 yd) silk ribbon no. 6 (pale pink),
4 mm (³⁄₁₆ in) wide

3 m (3.3 yd) silk ribbon no. 90 (pale blue),
4 mm (³⁄₁₆ in) wide

2 m (2.2 yd) silk ribbon no. 34 (ecru), 4 mm
(³⁄₁₆ in) wide

1 skein DMC stranded cotton no. 503 (pale
green)

1 packet small pearls

ASSEMBLY MATERIALS

1 m (1.1 yd) pale blue French chenille fringing

1 Cut out a piece of dupion silk measuring
24 cm (9½ in) square.

2 Trace the design onto the centre of the
fabric in pencil.

3 Stitch the cherub onto the fabric using 2
strands of ecru DMC.

4 Make 8 small ribbon roses using the pale
pink double-sided satin ribbon. Secure into
place using 2 strands of ecru DMC.

5 Using the photograph as a guide, embroider
the pink French knots and buds using the
pale pink silk ribbon.

6 Make 8 small ribbon roses, first using the
pale blue silk ribbon and then using the ecru
silk ribbon. Add a rosebud to the tip of the
arrow.

7 Fill in the greenery using 2 strands of the
pale green DMC. Start with a calyx at
the base of each French knot and bud, and
continue in long stem stitch for stems.
Fill in any leaves with leaf stitch.

8 To form the bunches of grapes, place
the first pearl in the hole on the tips of
the cherub's wings. Thread the pearls
individually with ecru cotton, layering
them as you go to create a bunch of grapes.

9 See pages 159–161 for finishing and making
up the cushion.

Finished cushion measures 22 cm (8½ in) square.
Tracing appears on page 157.

Victorian Cameo Heart Cushion

Because it is so small and delicate, this cushion is like a piece of fine porcelain. Here it's displayed within a richly lined cabinet along with a collection of precious porcelain pieces. The beautiful silk image of a young woman is appliquéd to a piece of pink moiré taffeta by finely embroidering lots of ribbons, fine wools, stranded cottons and silk threads to form a frame of different flowers. A tracery of gold ribbon completes the effect.

50 cm (20 in) square dusty pink moiré taffeta

silk cameo picture

1 ball cotton wool

2 m (2.2 yd) silk ribbon no. 178 (light plum),
   4 mm ($^3/_{16}$ in) wide

4 m (4.4 yd) silk ribbon no. 56 (green-gold),
   4 mm ($^3/_{16}$ in) wide

2 m (2.2 yd) silk ribbon no. 163 (dusty pink),
   4 mm ($^3/_{16}$ in) wide

4 m (4.4 yd) silk ribbon no. 6 (pale pink), 4 mm
   ($^3/_{16}$ in) wide

2 m (2.2 yd) silk ribbon no. 90 (pale blue), 4 mm
   ($^3/_{16}$ in) wide

1 skein DMC stranded cotton no. 320
   (mid-green)

1 skein DMC stranded cotton no. 726 (yellow)

1 skein DMC stranded cotton no. 819 (pale pink)

1 skein each DMC stranded cotton no. 341 and
   342 (cornflower blue)

1 skein DMC stranded cotton no. 3013 (antique
   green)

1 skein DMC stranded cotton no. 3688 (rose
   pink)

1 skein DMC stranded cotton no. 602 (bright
   pink)

1 skein DMC stranded cotton no. 3078 (lemon)

1 skein DMC stranded cotton no. 3042 or 211
   (mauve)

1 skein DMC stranded cotton no. 370 (bronze
   green)

1 m (1.1 yd) bronze cord

25 cm (10 in) dusty pink velvet ribbon, 10 mm
   ($^3/_8$ in) wide

2 m (2.2 yd) silk ribbon no. 5 or 6 (pale pink),
   7 mm ($^1/_3$ in) wide

1   Cut out a heart-shaped piece of moiré
taffeta (the watermark running vertically)
measuring approximately 24 cm (9½ in)
square. Trace the design onto the centre of
the heart in pencil.

2   Tack half of the silk cameo onto the centre
and pad lightly with cotton wool. Stitch the
remaining sides closed.

3   Using a variety of all the 4 mm-wide silk
ribbons, embroider a chain of daisies inside
and outside the edge of the circle. Alternate
the colours as you go.

4   Using the photograph as a guide, fill in the
centre of the circle using all of the DMC
colours in all of the flower stitches. Use all
6 strands to give the embroidery texture.

5   Lay down the bronze cord in the shape of
the bows and tack down with 2 strands of
the bronze green DMC.

6   Embroider sprays of French knots on the
tails of the bow using the pink 4 mm-wide
silk ribbon.

7   Fill in the greenery with the green DMCs,
using all 6 strands in leaf and stem stitches.

8   Make a ribbon rose using the dusty pink
velvet ribbon, and place it at the bottom of
the circle. Secure into place with 2 strands
of pale pink DMC.

9   Using the pale pink 7 mm-wide silk ribbon,
make 9 ribbon roses and position onto the
design. Place 5 at the top of the circle and 2
at either side of the velvet rose. Secure with
2 strands of pale pink DMC.

10 See pages 159–161 for finishing and making
up the cushion.

Finished cushion measures 22 cm (8½ in) square. Tracing appears on page 157.

My Friend Beverley's Bow Cushion

The hand-painted screen of cherubs amidst swirling clouds and trailing roses by Jane Devine makes a suitably hand-some backdrop for this cushion. Its embroidered bow – surrounded by fine cotton and ribbon embroidery – was partly inspired by the ornate bows on the hand-carved Italian photo frame on the side table.

136 | Finished cushion measures 15 × 23 cm (6 × 9 in). Tracing appears on page 157.

EMBROIDERY MATERIALS

18 × 27 cm (7 × 10½ in) square cream dupion silk

2 skeins ecru DMC stranded cotton

2 m (2.2 yd) silk ribbon no. 161 (dusky apricot), 4 mm (³⁄₁₆ in) wide

1 m (1.1 yd) silk ribbon no. 156 (cream), 4 mm (³⁄₁₆ in) wide

1 skein DMC stranded cotton no. 738 (dusky apricot)

1 skein DMC stranded cotton no. 3033 (deep ecru)

1 skein DMC stranded cotton no. 3011 (antique green)

1 skein DMC stranded cotton no. 3012 (antique green)

ASSEMBLY MATERIALS

3 × 8 × 40 cm (3 × 16 in) strips cream pleated dupion silk

1 Cut out a piece of dupion silk measuring 16 × 25 cm (6 × 10 in).

2 Trace the design onto the centre of the fabric in pencil.

3 Using 3 strands of ecru DMC, embroider the bow design in satin stitch. Satin stitch over the join of the bow twice to create a raised knot.

4 Embroider 6 ribbon daisies using the dusky apricot silk ribbon. Use the same ribbon to embroider the 3 buds in the posy above the centre of the bow.

5 Using the cream silk ribbon, embroider the 4 ribbon daisies at the tails of the bow.

6 Embroider the 4 large cotton daisies on the tails of the bow using 2 strands of the dusky apricot DMC. Embroider the 2 smaller cotton daisies using the deep ecru DMC.

7 Using 2 strands of deep ecru DMC, embroider the 2 grub roses on the tails of the bow. Embroider the buds and French knots in the same colour, using the photograph as a guide.

8 Embroider the French knots above the centre of the bow using 2 strands of dusky apricot DMC. Repeat, using the ecru DMC to complete the posy.

9 Make French knots to act as stamens at the centre of the ribbon daisies using the ecru DMC.

10 Thread a strand of each green DMC through a needle to sew the greenery. Use leaf stitch for the leaves around the ribbon daisies and a single French knot for the stamens in the centres of the cotton daisies. Connect all the remaining French knots and buds to the bow using French knots for the calyxes and long stem stitches for the stems.

11 See pages 159–161 for finishing and making up the cushion.

Pure elegance, pure romance.

Parisian Lace Cushion

The Parisian Lace Cushion was inspired by velvet flowers I bought in Paris. A dear

friend, the late Paddy Hornsby, gave me the antique lace and I wanted to find a way of

using them together. I laid down the lace on a piece of dupion silk, then edged them

with fine silk ribbons. Clusters of roses caught in bows were added, and the cushion

trimmed with more lace. The effect of this cream-on-cream finish is quite bridal, and

I can imagine the design being transferred to a wedding gown.

EMBROIDERY MATERIALS

30 cm (12 in) square cream quilted dupion silk

1 m (1.1 yd) narrow cream lace

1 skein ecru DMC stranded cotton

2.5 m (2.7 yd) silk ribbon no. 161 (coffee), 4 mm ($^3/_{16}$ in) wide

1 skein DMC stranded cotton no. 3047 (pale gold)

3 m (3.3 yd) silk ribbon no. 161 (coffee), 7 mm ($^1/_3$ in) wide

cream velvet flowers

green velvet leaves

1 skein DMC stranded cotton no. 733 (olive green)

2 m (2.2 yd) silk ribbon no. 56 (olive green), 7 mm ($^1/_3$ in) wide

ASSEMBLY MATERIALS

2.5 m (2.7 yd) wide cream lace

1   Cut out a piece of quilted dupion silk measuring 26 × 24 cm (10 × 9½ in).

2   Using the photograph as a guide, lay the strips of narrow lace onto the panels and tack down with 2 strands of ecru DMC.

3   Edge the panels of lace using the coffee 4 mm-wide silk ribbon. Secure the silk ribbon by embroidering French knots on the corner of each diamond with 6 strands of pale gold DMC.

4   Make 13 small ribbon roses using the coffee 7 mm-wide silk ribbon.

5   Using the diagram as a guide, position the velvet flowers and leaves. Secure into place with 4 strands of olive green DMC by embroidering calyxes and stems.

6   Using the coffee 7 mm-wide silk ribbon, embroider the buds in leaf stitch.

7   Embroider the ribbon leaves using the olive green 7 mm-wide silk ribbon.

8   Add the remaining calyxes and stems using 4 strands of olive green DMC.

9   Using the remaining coffee 7 mm-wide silk ribbon, embroider the 2 ribbon bows.

10   Stitch the ribbon roses into place using 2 strands of pale gold DMC.

11   See pages 159–161 for finishing and making up the cushion.

Finished cushion measures 24 × 22 cm (9½ × 8½ in). Tracing appears on page 158.

Cream Wreath on Moiré Taffeta Cushion

My daughter Charlotte made this cushion for me as a present, so it is very special. She designed it herself on some off-white taffeta, stitching on a circle of stems and leaves in pale green silk and stranded cotton, and finally adding clusters of white ribbon roses. It's finished with a generous taffeta frill. The cushion works equally well in a living area or in a bedroom. It certainly looks very refined on this gilded salon chair.

EMBROIDERY MATERIALS

75 cm (29½ in) square cream moiré taffeta

2 m (2.2 yd) bridal white double-sided satin
ribbon, 10 mm (³⁄₈ in) wide

1 skein ecru DMC stranded cotton

1 skein DMC stranded cotton no. 104 (pale
green)

1   Cut out a 22 cm (8½ in) square of moiré
taffeta.

2   Trace the design onto the centre of the
fabric in pencil.

3   Make 13 ribbon roses using the white
10 mm-wide double-sided satin ribbon.

4   Embroider all of the French knots using all
6 strands of ecru DMC.

5   Using the photograph as a guide, position
the roses and secure using 2 strands of ecru
DMC.

6   Using all 6 strands of the pale green DMC,
embroider the leaves around the ribbon roses
in leaf stitch.

7   Starting with a calyx at the base of each
French knot in the circle, create the wreath
effect by using all 6 strands of pale green
DMC in long stem stitches.

8   Again, using all 6 strands of pale green
DMC, connect the bunches of French knots
back to the roses using stem stitch.

9   See pages 159–161 for finishing and making
up the cushion.

Finished cushion measures 20 cm (8 in) square. Tracing appears on page 158.

Tracings

ENLARGE ALL TRACINGS TO 142%.

Girl with Cavalier Damask Cushion

Victorian Oyster Cushion
with Pearl Crest

Bronze Filigree Basket with
Poirot Roses Cushion

Antique Gold Cushion

Shimmering Rose Silk Cushion

Hanging Basket of Roses

Framed Cream Organza Rose Posy

Fuchsia Velvet Rose Cushion

Polka Dot Posy Cushion

Mona Lisa Cushion

Pink Florentine Cushion

Odenile Striped Cushion

Silver Posy Cushion

French Blue Velvet Rose Cushion

Matching French Blue Cushion

Julia's Rose Cushion

Antique Velvet Garland Cushion

Ivana Trump Cushion

Cream Carnation Posy Cushion

Ribbons and Bows Cushion

Cherub Dancing on Rosebuds

Posy on Blue-and-White
Striped Cushion

Ring of Roses Cushion

Cherub with Grapes Cushion

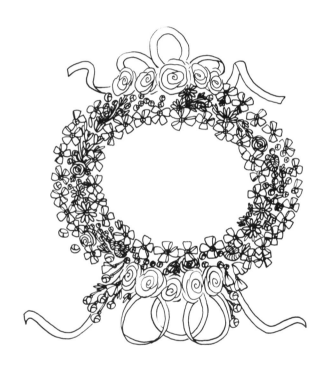

Victorian Cameo Heart Cushion

My Friend Beverley's Bow Cushion

Parisian Lace Cushion

Cream Wreath on Moiré Taffeta Cushion

Equipment

The following information is useful for those who wish to finish and make up their own cushions; however, you may prefer to take your work to a professional who will finish and make it up for you.

SEWING MACHINE

An expensive sewing machine is not necessary to complete the projects in this book as the only machine stitches required are straight and zigzag stitches.

To give a tailored and professional look to finished cushions I recommend that you use a zip, although a velcro fastener, buttons, press studs, stud tape or ribbons can also be used. A zipper foot is essential for inserting a zip neatly, and all sewing machines come with zipper feet. It takes practice to put in a zip, so before embarking on your first project it is a good idea to practise on an odd remnant of fabric.

A gathering foot is used for frills and ruching. Some sewing machines have a gathering foot included with the accessories, but if your machine does not have a gathering foot, you may purchase one from your local sewing-machine dealer. If this accessory is not available, a similar effect can be achieved by adjusting the stitch length and slightly loosening the tension.

MACHINE NEEDLES

For very delicate, lightweight fabrics such as organza or satin, use a size 10 or 12 machine needle, or else the needle will make holes in the fabric and pull the threads.

For calico, chintz, damask, and moiré and woollen fabrics, use a size 14 needle. For heavy fabrics such as tweed and tapestry, use a size 16 or 18 needle.

FABRICS

While you may choose from a seemingly limitless range of fabrics to make the cushions in this book, I recommend fabrics with a firm handle. Anything that is too lightweight will eventually lose its shape and appear limp and unattractive when finished. Dress fabrics may be used, but they often have too soft a finish to make a successful cushion. When planning a new project, try putting together fabrics of different weight and texture – it will ensure a far more interesting result!

Buy the best quality materials you can find. Some of the projects in this book use expensive fabrics, but only minimally. It is worth paying more for good-quality fabric if you are going to put a lot of time and effort into a piece of work.

Calico is an inexpensive material which often has many faults in the fabric. Buy it from the home furnishings department rather than from the dress fabrics section: the home furnishing calico is a lot wider and more economical. Because strong finishes are used in the fabric production, you will find that prolonged use of calico on a sewing machine will result in both a blunt needle and a machine that needs oiling. Wash the fabric before use and drip dry, as calico tends to crease badly in a dryer.

Damask fabrics are now available in a range of colours. Watch out for old damask tablecloths in antique shops or at garage sales – they may have stains or holes in places, but they may yield just enough fabric for a small cushion.

When planning a new project, build up a colour storyboard. Attach to a manila folder some wall-colour samples, and swatches of carpet and other furnishing fabrics from the room you intend to embellish. Then start collecting fabrics and trims that you can use for your next cushion. This way you can avoid expensive mistakes and take advantage of fabric sales by looking for specific colours and textures to fit in with your colour scheme.

YARNS

I used Paterna yarn tapestry wool for all the woollen embroidery in this book. Paterna yarn is 100-per-cent virgin wool, has a soft lustre and is available in a wonderful range of colours. It is a three-ply yarn, which means that it can be separated into single strands as required.

The cotton yarns used are from the DMC range. The DMC colour range is extensive and the quality is excellent.

RIBBONS

I recommend you use only pure silk ribbons for all ribbon embroidery. Relatively inexpensive synthetic ribbons are available, but silk ribbons are more pliable and manageable, and produce first-class results.

NEEDLES

A chenille needle has a very large eye and a sharp point, and has been used for almost all the embroidery in this book. Chenille needles are sold in packs ranging from size 18 to 24.

Use a size 24 chenille needle for ribbon embroidery. For finer embroidery, try the size 9 embroidery needle by Birch.

BRAIDS AND TASSELS

There is an enormous variety of decorative trimmings available. Many are costly, so it is very important to select the braid or tassel trim before you select the fabric – not the other way round. This is particularly important when you are planning a piece of embroidery: it is easy to blend the embroidery colours with a braid, but it is often difficult to find the right colours in a braid after you have finished the project.

If the braid or tassel trim is wide, make sure

you allow enough depth on the edge of the cushion so that the braid doesn't flop over the edge. Be careful when machining the braid so that you don't catch any pieces in the seam.

CUSHION INSERTS

Buy or make a larger insert than the actual size of the finished cushion to give it a firm appearance. For instance, a 35 cm (14 in) insert should be used for a 30 cm (12 in) cushion. This also helps protect the cushion from losing its shape through wear and tear.

For embroidered cushions, the insert should be the same size as the cushion, otherwise the texture of the embroidery will become too taut.

Standard cushion inserts are readily available, but when unusual sizes and shapes are required, for example heart-shaped, round or very small cushions, it is necessary to make your own. Again, make the insert a fraction larger than the actual size of the cushion.

CUSHION FILLINGS

Forget about the old stocking routine – these days, a wide variety of fillings is available from craft shops. The most popular is polyester fibrefill, which comes in many weights. There is a craft fibrefill (used mainly for stuffing toys), which is a heavier weight but which is also ideal for filling cushions.

Synthetic foam is widely available but is not recommended unless it is mixed with feathers to break down the bulk of the foam.

Feathers are still used for cushions that require an antique old-world look, but tend to be floppy and give a lived-in appearance. I recommend that you do any feather stuffing out of doors on a windless day – and lock up the dog!

Before putting a filled insert into a finished cushion, knead the insert with your hands, working the filling right into the corners so that the centre is almost hollow. Fold the insert in your hand and place it inside the cushion from corner to corner.

When making an insert for a heart-shaped or a round cushion, fill the insert slowly. Put in the filling piece by piece, making sure that it is evenly distributed and that there are no lumps and bumps. Fold the insert in half, pushing the filling into all the corners.

Stitch Glossary

BULLION STITCH

Bullion stitch is like a French knot, but it produces a fan-like shape rather than a rosette. It is one of the most difficult stitches and requires quite a bit of practice to perfect.

1   Bring the needle through the top of the middle stitch (this is the length of your stitch). Take the needle through the bottom of the stitch and insert the tip of the needle exactly at the top of the stitch again. Do not pull the needle all the way through.

2   Wind the thread around the needle 12 times.

3   Hold the wound threads tightly between your thumb and index finger and pull the needle all the way until all the loose thread is through. Tighten up and put the needle back through the base of the middle stitch.

4   Repeat steps 1 to 3 for the remaining stitches. For the 2 stitches either side of the centre stitch, wind the thread around the needle 10 times. For the 2 outer stitches, wind the thread 8 times.

CALYX AND STEM

1   Bring the needle through the back of the fabric at the base of the flower.

2   Take the needle from right to left through the base of the flower. Don't pull the thread all the way through.

3   Leave an open loop of thread at the right of the flower. Take the needle through the back of the loop from the left-hand side of the flower.

4   Pull down to form a figure-of-eight knot.

5   Embroider a long stitch to form the stem. It's best to have a slightly curved stem.

6   Secure the stem in place with a couching stitch halfway down.

CARNATION

1　Take a 1 m (1.1 yd) length of ribbon. Fold the ribbon twice at the end and stitch down with 2 blanket stitches using 2 strands of DMC cotton.

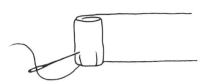

2　Using a concertina folding method, fold the ribbon 5 times and secure at the base with 2 blanket stitches.

3　Fold the remaining ribbon with inverted pleats, securing each pleat with blanket stitches.

4　Fold the pleated length of ribbon clockwise around the pleated centre, making sure the bottom is even and flat. Secure with DMC cotton.

DAISY STITCH

The daisy is made from a series of straight stitches in a spoked-wheel pattern. Start the daisy petal by bringing up the needle at point A and inserting it at point B, the centre of the daisy. (This makes it easier to get the petals evenly spaced.)

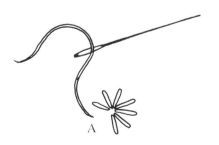

FRENCH KNOT

1 Bring the needle up through the fabric at point A.

2 Make a small stitch from right to left underneath point A. Pull the needle through to form a loop with the thread.

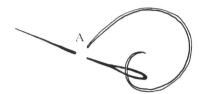

3 Coming from around the front of the loop, take the needle around the back and through the loop. Pull the thread to make a small half-knot.

4 Take the needle through point B and pull loosely to form a small neat knot that lies flush with the material.

LEAF STITCH

The leaf stitch is a combination of three straight stitches. The centre stitch is the longest stitch with 2 slightly shorter stitches on either side. This stitch is also used for sewing buds.

1 Bring the needle up through the fabric at point A. Make a straight stitch to point B.

2 Bring the needle up through point A again. Make a slightly shorter straight stitch to point C.

3 Come up through point A again and make a small stitch to point D. Finish off at the back of the fabric.

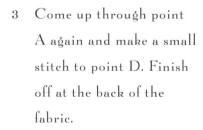

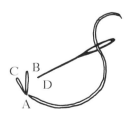

PEONY ROSE

1   To make the centre of the peony rose, make a ribbon rose (see page 168).

2   To make the inner petals, cut out a piece of ribbon about 4 cm (1½ in) long. Fold down the corners, and with short running stitches tack along the bottom of the ribbon with one strand of DMC cotton.

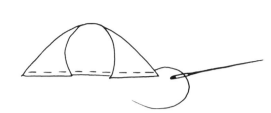

3   Pull the thread to gather the ribbon. Try to keep the centre of the petal straight as you gather the edges. Make about 5 petals and set aside.

4   To make the outer petals, follow steps 2 and 3, making the petals longer as you go. The very outer petals should be about 10 cm (4 in) long before they are gathered.

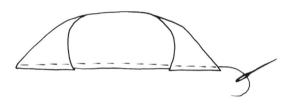

5   Starting with the smallest petals, stitch the petals around the ribbon rose with the folds facing outwards. Overlap each petal and anchor at the base of the rose with 2 strands of DMC cotton.

6   Keep overlapping the petals, finishing with the largest petals. Make sure the base of the petals are flush with the base of the centre rose.

NEW ROSE

This variation on the peony rose uses a mixture of ribbons rather than a double-sided satin ribbon.

1   Using a combination of 2 ribbons, make a carnation (see page 164) as the centre of this new rose. Sheer organza and taffeta or satin ribbons work well together.

2   To make the outer petals, follow steps 3 to 5 of the instructions for the peony rose, alternating the ribbons as you go.

RIBBON BOW

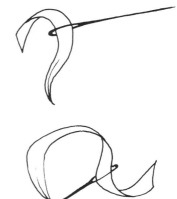

1   Bring the needle up through the back of the fabric.

2   Form a loop with the ribbon by making a small stitch to the right.

3   Keep the ribbon flat and even to form the right loop of the bow. Angle the loop down slightly for a more natural look.

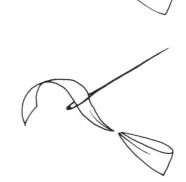

4   Bring the needle up through the fabric slightly to the left of the first loop. Repeat to form the left loop.

5   To form the centre of the bow, bring the needle through the top of the join in the bow and make a small vertical stitch. Be sure to keep the ribbon raised and even.

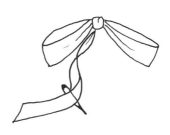

6   To form the tails, bring the needle through the base of the knot and extend to the desired length. Twist the ribbon once or twice and take the needle through to the back of the fabric.

7   To make the other tail, start at the bottom of the tail, pull through and extend it to the desired length. Twist the ribbon once or twice, and finish off at the base of the knot.

RIBBON LEAVES

Make these in the same way as the ribbon rosebuds (see page 169), but without the padding. Add them to the flower, hiding their bases under the flower.

RIBBON ROSE

1   Fold the end of the ribbon and roll 5 times. Secure halfway up the core to ensure it doesn't unroll.

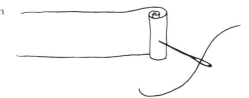

2   Holding the centre in your right hand and the remaining ribbon in your left, turn down the top edge of the ribbon away from the centre.

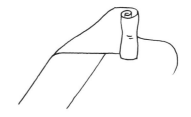

3   Roll the centre clockwise and the folded-down ribbon will form a petal. Secure with a few small stitches.

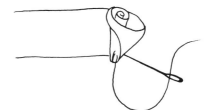

4   Repeat step 3 until you achieve the size of the ro

5   Hold the rose in your left hand with the remaining ribbon to the right. Fold the ribbon on an angle.

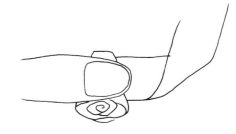

6   Fold the angled ribbon over the rose to the left and stitch down with DMC cotton. Cut the remaining ribbon off at the base of the rose.

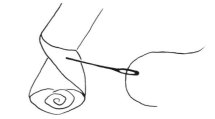

RIBBON ROSEBUD

1   Take a 10 cm (4 in) length of ribbon and fold at one end to form a loop. Using one strand of DMC cotton, tack a running stitch across the front of the ribbon. Do not catch the back of the loop.

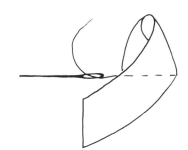

2   Pull the thread to gather the ribbon and wind the thread around the gathered middle. Secure with a stitch through the middle.

3   Turn the bud over. Fold the ribbon tail in half lengthwise. Fold up to the base of the bud.

4   Tack a running stitch around the edge of the ribbon at the back of the bud. Tuck the folded ribbon tail into the hollow bud and pull the thread to close.

5   Finish off by securing with a few small stitches.

ROSETTE STITCH

This is a miniature stem stitch worked in an ever-decreasing circle. Make a series of small stem stitches in a circle, and keep working round and round in an inwards direction. Keep the stitches loose and as close together as possible to give the rosette height. To finish off at the centre, make a small loop to look like a rosebud and take the thread to the back of the fabric. Fasten off.

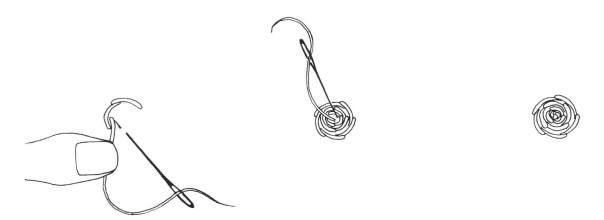

SATIN STITCH

This is a basic stitch used for filling bows, ovals, heart shapes and initials. It is very important to keep the stitches even and loose as tight stitching makes the fabric pucker and spoils the whole effect. Satin stitch is just straight stitch worked closely together.

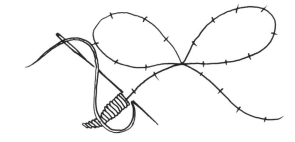

STEM STITCH

This is basically a long straight stitch used for sewing the stems and leaves of most flowers. It is also used to form circles and ovals.

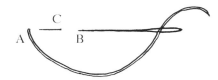
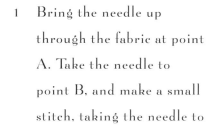
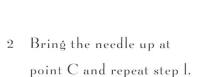

1 Bring the needle up through the fabric at point A. Take the needle to point B, and make a small stitch, taking the needle to point C.

2 Bring the needle up at point C and repeat step 1. Make a small stitch at point D and finish at point E.

3 Continue until you have the desired length of stitches, working from left to right.

Sewing Techniques

FRENCH SEAMS

French seams are used on pillowcases and where a strong seam is required. They give a neat, tailored finish.

Technique

1 Join two straight edges together, right sides together. Machine stitch.

2 Trim the seam very close to the stitching. Press open.

3 Turn the seam over and stitch again, enclosing the raw edges. Press.

FRILLS

I provide specific measurements for frill size in each of the projects in this book. The technique for each is the same.

Technique

1 Cut three strips of fabric (or sometimes four for a very full frill).

2 Join the fabric strips together with three (or four) seams to make one continuous frill. Iron the seams open. Fold the frill in half lengthwise with the right side out. Press.

3 Attach a gathering foot to the machine or change to long gathering stitch, and gather the frill to fit the cushion's circumference.

4 Divide the gathered frill into four quarters (for each side of a square cushion) and mark with a pin. Pin each quarter of the frill to the appropriate quarter of the cushion front (whatever the shape), dividing the gathers evenly. Machine stitch right around the frill.

5 Machine stitch across the top of the zip. Change to the zipper foot, open the zip and place it facing downwards behind the frill, on the front of the cushion. Baste, and then machine stitch close to the teeth of the zip. Close the zip (which should still be facing downwards).

6 Place the back of the cushion on top of the frill and machine stitch across the other side of the zip and on the three sides.

7 Neaten the edges and turn through.

PIPING

A wide variety of piping cords is available, varying in widths from size 0 to 14. The piping cord is covered with material, always cut on the cross.

Technique

1 To cover the cording, measure the amount of cording to fit the circumference of the cushion, allowing a little extra for turning corners. Cut a piece of fabric on the cross to cover the cording.

2 Change to the zipper foot, place the cording along the middle of the wrong side of the fabric. Using the zipper foot, join both sides of the fabric together with the cording inside as a loose casing.

3 Take the front of the cushion, place the piping on the chalk seam line and stitch close to the piping edge. Leave the machine needle in the fabric and snip into the corner before turning.

4 To finish off narrow piping, overlap the ends and machine stitch. For wide piping, hand stitch the overlap.

RUCHING

The Victorians loved ruching – their petticoats, dresses and hats often had ruched edgings – and they introduced ruching to pillows and upholstery. A ruched edging never crushes, always keeps its shape and can provide a striking change of texture, pattern and colour. A tightly gathered fabric gives a formal, luxurious effect, and it emphasises the outline of the cushion.

Adding ruching to the edge of a cushion is really just adding a closely gathered frill which has cording inside it to give the edge some shape. Cording is available from haberdashery shops in a variety of sizes, similar to those for piping. The larger cordings make the most im-

pact. Once the technique of adding frills (see page 171) has been mastered, ruching is a piece of cake!

Technique

1 To work out the amount of cording you will need, measure the circumference of the cushion and add 18 cm (7 in) to allow for joins and corners.

2 Join the cording by crossing then hand sewing the ends together. Tape over the join with masking tape.

3 Make a narrow frill (see page 171), then insert the cording into the narrow frill edging. Using the gathering foot or long machine stitch, gather the frill with the cording inside to fit the circumference of the cushion. Do not press.

ZIPS

Rather than leaving the zip until last, it is best to sew it in at an early stage before the back section of the cushion is attached. Always buy a zip that is about 5 cm (2 in) smaller than the actual size of the cushion. This prevents the zip from getting caught in the corners of the cushion when turning through. It also results in less bulk, particularly in a cushion with rounded corners.

Before basting the zip into the cushion, machine stitch the tops of the zip together. This will prevent both unevenness and the zip breaking apart during sewing. Inexperienced sewers should always baste the zip into place before machine sewing.

Zips are usually placed on the bottom of a square or oblong cushion where it sits on a couch or chair. Heart-shaped, round and oval cushions, or bolsters have the zip located in the centre of the back.

A double welt is used when the zip is placed in the centre of the back of the cushion, rather than at the bottom. A double-welt seam is one where the zip is stitched down on both sides, rather than only on one.

Technique

For any cushion where the zip is placed on the bottom:

1 Machine stitch across the top of the zip.

2 Change to the zipper foot, open the zip and place it face down behind the frill or piping on one side of the cushion.

3 Baste the zip into place and then machine stitch close to the teeth of the zip. Close the zip (still facing downwards), allowing a small opening on the seam for turning through.

4 Turn the work to the right side, and baste the other side of the zip to the back of the cushion. Machine stitch.

For heart-shaped, round and oval cushions, or bolsters (using a double-welt seam):

1 Machine stitch across the top of the zip.

2 Change to the zipper foot. Make sure the zip is closed. Place the zip behind the fabric and machine stitch on both sides.

AN ANTIQUE EFFECT FOR PICTURE INSERTS

Technique

For cushions requiring an aged picture insert such as the Pink Florentine Cushion (see pages 60–63):

1 Soak picture in a weak bleach solution ($\frac{1}{2}$ cup bleach to 2 litres water) overnight until picture begins to fade.

2 Wash picture thoroughly several times in hot, soapy water. Sprinkle the wrong side with Ajax and scrub on the right side with a stiff brush. Wash thoroughly and rinse well.

3 To give the fabric a sepia tone, make a weak solution of light brown Gilseal fabric dye and soak the picture for half an hour. Rinse and wring tightly. Leave picture for several hours. Smooth flat and allow to dry.

Materials and Kit Information

All the materials in this book and in my two previous books are available in kit form from my boutique. I conduct classes there, as well as at The Craft Cottage in Mount Waverley and Bustle and Bows in Surrey Hills and Malvern. I also travel across Australia and overseas to teach. For those who don't have the patience, the time or the desire to take up embroidery themselves, I still make and sell cushions on request.

SUPPLIERS

Kaye Pyke

1st floor 359 Bay Street Port Melbourne Victoria 3207

Tel (03) 9646 3540 Fax (03) 9646 3082

Croyden Galleries

359 Bay Street Port Melbourne Victoria 3207

Tel (03) 9646 3540

Chinatique

505 High Street Prahran East Victoria 3181

Tel (03) 9510 9820

Chyka Keebaugh

Tel (03) 9822 3663